DAVID WHITWELL

ESSAYS ON ITALIAN AND SPANISH MUSIC OF THE BAROQUE

PHILOSOPHY AND PERFORMANCE PRACTICE

WHITWELL BOOKS

Essays on Italian and Spanish Music of the Baroque: Philosophy and Performance Practice
Dr. David Whitwell

Copyright © 2015 David Whitwell
All rights reserved.
Published in the United States of America.
These essays were originally written between 2000–2010.

Cover image: *Fontana di trevi Figuras de Neptuno y Salebridad* by Miguel Hermoso Cuesta, 2011

ISBN-13 978-1-936512-82-9

Whitwell Publishing
Austin, TX 78701
WWW.WHITWELLPUBLISHING.COM

Contents

1 On Defining the Italian Baroque — 9
2 Thoughts on the Beginning of Italian Opera — 23
3 Italian Views on Baroque Performance Practice — 37
4 Kircher on Music — 55
5 On Court Music of the Italian Baroque — 67
6 On Civic and Military Music of the Italian Baroque — 79
7 On Church Music of the Italian Baroque — 87
8 Thoughts on Music of the Spanish Baroque — 105

Bibliography — 123

About the Author — 133

About the Editor — 137

I want to express my appreciation for my colleague, Craig Dabelstein of Brisbane, Australia, for his contribution to this volume. His own musicianship, broad education and skill in editing is responsible for thus preserving my essays. Any reader who places value in having these essays in his library is in his debt.

1
On Defining the Italian Baroque

I never met with any man that suffered his passions to hurry him away so much whilst he was playing on the violin as the famous Arcangelo Corelli, whose eyes will sometimes turn as red as fire; his countenance will be distorted, his eyeballs roll as in an agony, and he gives in so much to what he is doing that he doth not look like the same man.[1]

[1] Oliver Strunk, "François Raguenet, *Comparison between the French and Italian Music* (1702)," *The Musical Quarterly* 32, no. 3 (Jul., 1946): 419fn.

NOTHING, IN OUR VIEW, so clearly defines the Baroque as the above eyewitness description of Corelli. How far removed is this understanding of music from the old Catholic Scholastic dogma which held that music was a branch of mathematics! Between these two poles stands the Renaissance which, in music, symbolizes the rediscovery of the ancient truth that the purpose of music is to communicate feeling. The real story of the Baroque, in music, is an enthusiastic embrace of emotions in music and a fervent search for how this happens through music.

In the seventeenth century Italy was still not Italy. One of Europe's oldest civilizations remained, since the fall of the Roman Empire, a series of individual kingdoms, principalities, duchies, city-republics and the land controlled by the pope. Spain, Austria, France, and the popes kept the peninsula in a continual state of conflict. That out of this had come the Renaissance in the fifteenth and sixteenth centuries is remarkable.

One is tempted to suppose that, after the extraordinary leadership of Italy in the arts during the Renaissance, she needed a period of rest. A more objective view might see the influence of a colder intellectual climate caused by the Church after the Council of Trent.[2] This is most apparent in painting, where nudes were no longer allowed and only the fervent pleas of a group of artists prevented the Pope Clement VIII from having Michelangelo's *Last Judgment* completely painted over. In music, the noble patrons turned to entertainment and great numbers of distinguished musicians left for other countries, making Italian music important everywhere except in Italy.

We can see how strong these old-fashioned conservative feelings were, and how they contrasted with the progressive ideas of the Baroque, in a little squabble in Bologna in the middle of the seventeenth century. This incident began with the hiring of Don Mauritio Cazzati as *maestro di cappella* at the cathedral, S. Petronio in 1657,[3] and his institution of a series of reforms.[4] This effort at reform was met, by the faithful members of the capella under the leadership of the deputy organist, Arresti, with resistance, resignations and remonstrations. Among the latter is a *Dialogo*, a document circulated for the purpose of personally attacking Cazzati. Among the criticisms, some are especially enlightening regarding contemporary practice and values.

> He writes sophisticated introductions to the "Gloria," "Credo," and "Laudate Pueri," which are not used in most chapels;
> He uses vocal soloists when he has 80 singers there;
> He teaches neither singing nor playing nor counterpoint, and never goes to the school, as is his duty, so that my son finds a way of life and a moral code which is totally unacceptable in this city;
> He does not know how to place or order the choirs;
> He does not know how to produce the voice and is afraid to sing without the organ, violone and trombone;
> He likes to take the credit for other people's compositions and distribute them as his own, even in printed editions; as he did ... when he distributed books around the place which said "Music by Mauritio Cazzati," when most of the compositions had been written by Don Lorenzo Perti;
> He does not know how to teach the sopranos, who are necessary for the service of the church—which it is his duty to

[2] The Inquisition remained a fearful part of the conservative Church climate. Monteverdi, in his letters, writes of having to go to great lengths to have his son (a doctor of medicine!) released from prison for having read a book which he did not realize was on the prohibited list.

[3] This "polemic" is discussed thoroughly in Ursula Brett, *Music and Ideas in Seventeenth Century Italy* (New York: Garland Publishing, 1989).

[4] Most of these dealt with the dress and discipline of the singers and are quoted in ibid., 58ff.

do—and concerning this, he has never crossed the threshold of the school to go and teach them;

Finally, he uses Bergamasks, Chaconnes and Ruggieri [as opposed to instrumental canzoni], and calls them Ritornelli.

What followed was a series of published tracts by both Cazzati defending himself and others attacking him. The attacks centered on criticism of Cazzati's own compositions for the church, which were made the object of a detailed search for examples where Cazzati did not follow the rules of sixteenth century church polyphony. Nowhere is this more clearly stated, than in one attack which summarized,

> That the whole [composition] is composed without mode, without reason, with little grace, less elegance, and is bereft of the laws and precepts of the respected Masters, from which one should not depart if one aims to follow the good rules of this mathematical science.

To not "follow the mathematical rules" was considered by such conservatives to be an indication that the composer was "lacking in moral and intellectual virtue." But there was a fundamental aesthetic question raised as well. One measure in Cazzati's composition was attacked for having a sixth above the bass.

> What melodious delight can a miserable sixth, devoid of counterpoint so that I find myself hissing, ever bring to the ear of the listener? Is it enough that music, in order to be beautiful, merely delights the sense of him who listens to it?

The implication here is that satisfaction is found in hearing the rules of musical grammar and not the music. The opinion was further strengthened by the suggestion that "the rules" were of divine inspiration, if not divine origin. To these claims, Cazzati answered, in effect, that it is the ear which judges music, not rules.

> However, you know, O reader, that the rules of music are not divine precepts, but human opinions and diverse, as may be seen from the printed books: and many virtuosi with printed works to their credit, have claimed to be not in error for the

reason that it is necessary to see whether a composition is pleasing. The one which is pleasing, then, can be said to be composed according to the rules; and the one which is not pleasing, even if it be composed in accordance with all the rules, is not good since it displeases—because music is made in order to please and not to displease.[5]

[5] Ibid., 107.

Among the writings of the Italian musicians of the Baroque one also finds numerous comments which reflect the great changes taking place in the practice of music. Italian humanists already in the sixteenth century, even before the generation of Palestrina, were condemning the old Church polyphonic style. Nevertheless, it is somewhat surprising to find Agostino Agazzari implying as early as 1607 that this style is "no longer in use," for as we know some composers would in fact continue to compose this older style of polyphonic church music until well into the eighteenth century.

> That kind of music is no longer in use, both because of the confusion and babel of the words, arising from the long and intricate imitations, and because it has no grace, for, with all the voices singing, one hears neither period nor sense, these being interfered with and covered up by imitations; indeed, at every moment, each voice has different words, a thing displeasing to men of competence and judgment ... Such compositions are good according to the rules of counterpoint, but they are at the same time faulty according to the rules of music that is true and good.[6]

[6] Agostino Agazzari, "On Playing upon a Bass in ... Consort," quoted in Oliver Strunk, *Source Readings in Music History* (New York: Norton, 1950), 430.

In this same work a comment by Agazzari reflects the growing preference for string instruments. This change in taste, which brought to an end centuries of domination by winds in art music, was due in part to the advance in the quality of the manufacture of string instruments during the seventeenth century and in part because of the interest of the humanists in the ancient Greek accounts of singing accompanied by strings. Of the wind instruments,

> I shall say nothing, because they are not used in good and pleasing consorts, because of their insufficient union with the stringed instruments and because of the variation produced

in them by the human breath, although they are introduced in great and noisy consorts.[7]

[7] Ibid., 425.

Perhaps more influential was the fact that at the same time, during the seventeenth century, the winds were going through a dramatic transformation, with the retirement of nearly all the Renaissance instruments and their replacement by the modern instruments. Clearly a long period ensued during which makers struggled with improvements and players struggled with having to learn entirely new instruments, resulting in complaints about such things as intonation. A typical example is found in Charles Burney, who maintains he heard Alessandro Scarlatti say, "My son, you know I hate wind instruments, they are never in tune."[8]

[8] Quoted in Robert Donnington, *The Interpretation of Early Music* (New York, 1964), 548.

Another change one finds in the highest levels of society during the Baroque concerns the participation of the noble. In the Renaissance the ability to perform was considered a mark of culture, but during the Baroque the noble generally became only the employer of musicians. Gasparini takes it for granted that the noble no longer has time for music. He makes this observation while reflecting that most experts consider three things necessary for the making of a musician: resolve, application and a good teacher. But even more important than these, he says, is a natural disposition. This, he says, is a gift of God and nature and cannot be otherwise obtained at any price.[9]

[9] Francesco Gasparini, *The Practical Harmonist at the Harpsichord* [1708], ed., Franks S. Stillings (New Haven: Yale School of Music, 1963), 9.

> There are an infinite number of nobles, gentlemen, ladies, and princes, who feel an inclination toward music, but should they start in, it is certain that, because of their customary preoccupation with studies of literature or other gentlemanly exercises, a generation, so to speak, would not suffice them to arrive at the playing of four notes.[10]

[10] Ibid., 10.

One manifestation of the new interest in emotions in music was a gradual realization that perhaps different emotions are appropriate to different venues. Hence there developed among some a tendency to categorize performance under three locales: theater, church and chamber. A typical example can be seen in Tosi, who argues for entirely separate aesthetic values according to whether the performance takes place in a church, the theater or in the chamber. His most detailed discussion of these distinctions occurs when he discusses the recitative.

> The recitative is of three kinds and ought to be taught in three different manners.
>
> The first, being used in churches, should be sung as becomes the sanctity of the place, which does not admit those wanton graces[11] of a lighter style; but requires some *Messa di Voce*, appoggiaturas and a noble majesty throughout …
>
> The second style is the theatrical, which … cannot be beautiful, if not expressed with that decorum with which princes speak, or those who know how to speak to princes.
>
> The third, which according to the opinion of the most judicious, touches the heart more than the other two, is called *Recitativo di Camera*. This requires a more peculiar skill, by reason of the words, which being, for the most part, adapted to move the strongest passions of the soul, require the teacher to give the student such a lively impression of them, that he may seem to be affected with them himself.[12]

Of course, the most immediate symbol of the Baroque was opera, the subject of the following chapter. The enormous popularity of the new opera form during the Baroque created an entirely new social phenomenon, the prima donna. Benedetto Marcello gives us a humorous view of the social status of the prima donna in his satirical account of "Theater in the Modern Style," of 1720. He observes that the composer must not object to the great fees paid the singers and must be content if he himself is paid no more than the trained bear. Also on the street he must walk a step behind the singers, especially the *castrati*. All this, because "his own reputation, credit, and interests are in their hands."[13]

In another passage, which reflects the new style of upper and lower line dominance, his recommendation that an impresario can economize on double basses is intended to be a humorous jab at the numerous contemporary theorists who stressed the importance of the bass line. Curiously, he adds, the double basses must be used for tuning.[14]

---

[11] By which he means improvisation!

[12] P. F. Tosi, *Observations on the Florid Song* (London: Wilcox, 1743), V.

[13] Benedetto Marcello, "Il treatro alla moda," quoted in Oliver Strunk, *Source Readings in Music History* (New York: Norton, 1950), 527ff. Marcello (b. 1686) was one of the most gifted composers of the Italian Baroque.

[14] Ibid., 530.

Finally, Marcello makes a subtle reference to the eighteenth century tendency for a court to expect its musicians, as most were indentured servants, to also work in other non-musical jobs (even Haydn had non-musical duties). Marcello recommends that in the printed program of an opera, the acknowledgment of the composer should read,

> The music is by the ever most celebrated Signor N. N., conductor of the orchestra, of concerts, of chamber concerts, dancing master, fencing master, etc., etc., etc., etc.[15]

[15] Ibid., 531.

The courts, nevertheless, were where the money was and Tosi offered singers the advice that they take advantage of visiting the many courts of Europe. Visit, he warns, but don't stay,

> For chains, though of gold, are still chains; and they are not all made of that precious metal. Besides, the several inconveniences of disgrace, mortifications, uncertainty and, above all, hindrance of study [are associated with serving a court].[16]

[16] P. F. Tosi, *Observations on the Florid Song*, VIII, xii.

But travel they did, in that perennial hope that the "grass is greener on the other side of the fence." Thus, Alessandro Scarlatti, in a letter of 1705 regarding his son, Domenico, announced,

> I am sending him away from Rome, because Rome offers no roof to Music, which lives here like a beggar.[17]

And, of course, the grass was not always greener, as Geminiani observed of London.

[17] Alessandro Scarlatti, letter to Prince Ferdinand de' Medici, May 30, 1705, quoted in Piero Weiss, *Letters of Composers Through Six Centuries* (Philadelphia: Chilton, 1967), 58.

> When I first came to London, which was thirty-four years ago, I found music in so thriving a state, that I had all the reason imaginable to suppose the growth would be suitable to the excellency of the soil.
> But I have lived to be most miserably disappointed; for though it cannot be said that there was any lack of encouragement, that encouragement was ill bestowed.
> The hand was more considered than the head; the performance than the composition; and hence it followed, that instead of laboring to cultivate a taste, which seemed to be all that was lacking, the public was content to nourish insipidity.[18]

[18] Francesco Geminiani, *A Treatise of Good Taste in the Art of Musick* [1749] (New York: Da Capo Press, 1969), 4.

The most far-reaching accomplishment by the late sixteenth century Italian humanists was the re-establishment of music's most natural purpose, the expression of feeling. They affected this through their philosophical criticism of the old mathematics-based polyphony and by creating modern opera as a demonstration of their aims. This purpose is clearly expressed, in 1600, by Emilio de' Cavalieri in the preface to his *Rappresentazione di Anima, et di Corpo,* where he states that his purpose is to "move the listener to different emotions, as pity, joy, tears, and laughter, and other similar emotions."[19] To help make this possible, by way of aiding the listener's hearing the singer, he recommends placing the orchestra behind a curtain and requests they perform without improvisation. It is particularly interesting that he recommends the orchestra members changing instruments, according to the *affetti,* a practice which would explain the very large list of instruments associated with Monteverdi's *Orfeo.*

Also with respect to hearing the singer, Cavalieri recommends performance in a hall seating no more than one thousand! Otherwise,

> If it is presented in very large halls it is not possible to hear all the words; and the singer would have to force his voice, which lessens the emotional effect; also, so much music with the words not being audible becomes tiresome.[20]

With regard to Cavalieri's preference to hide the orchestra behind a curtain, we should mention that Marco da Gagliano, in the preface to his *Dafne* of 1608, takes a different view.

> Make sure that the instruments that are to accompany the solo voices are located so that they can see the faces of the performers, in order that by hearing each other better they may perform together.[21]

Monteverdi, in 1638, makes an interesting general comment about the communication of emotions at present and most diplomatically criticizes the previous Church composers for not being emotional enough.

> I consider the principal passions or emotions of the soul to be three, namely, anger, serenity, and humility. The best

[19] Emilio de' Cavalieri, "Rappresentazione di Anima, et di Corpo," Preface, quoted in Carol MacClintock, *Readings in the History of Music in Performance* (Bloomington: Indiana University Press, 1979), 183.

[20] Ibid., 184.

[21] Ibid., 190.

philosophers affirm this; the very nature of our voice, with its high, low and middle ranges, shows it; and the art of music clearly manifests it in these three terms: agitated, soft and moderate. I have not been able to find an example of the agitated style in the works of past composers, but I have discovered many of the soft and moderate types.[22]

Angelo Berardi probably said it best, when he observed in 1681, "Music is the ruler of the passions of the soul."[23]

For the goals of the humanists to be manifested, of course, the first responsibility rested with the composer. One composer who was particularly sensitive to the listener, with respect to the new emphasis on the expression of emotions, was Monteverdi. In a letter of 1617, he recommends, for a court theatrical production, first of all a sinfonia to prepare the minds of the audience.[24] In another letter regarding a court theatrical work, he proposes that a character speak in a soft voice, which "will give me a chance to introduce to the senses a new kind of music, different from what has gone before."[25]

Marcello writes of a letter of 1711 that he has tried in his music to lend "more expression to the words" and refers to the earlier polyphonic style as having a "natural sterility."[26] Alessandro Scarlatti (1660–1725) expressed the same concern in a letter to his patron, Prince Ferdinand de' Medici. Speaking of his *Il Gran Tamerlano* (1706), Scarlatti relates that he tried to achieve, "naturalness and beauty, together with the expression of the passion with which the characters speak."[27] The latter, he said, "is the very most principal consideration and circumstance for moving and leading the mind of the listener to the diversity of sentiments that the various incidents of the plot of the drama unfold."

Agazzari, in his treatise on concerti, stresses that the instruments of the accompaniment must also share the responsibility of expressing feelings. "When there are words," he says, "they must be clothed with that suitable harmony which arouses or conveys some passion."[28]

As might be expected, there were some who were concerned with the fervent enthusiasm for the communication

[22] Monteverdi, "Madrigali guerrieri ed amorosi" (1638), preface, quoted in Sam Morgenstern, *Composers on Music* (New York: Pantheon, 1956), 22.

[23] Angelo Berardi, *Ragionamenti Musicali* (Bologna, 1681), 87.

[24] Letter to Alessandro Striggio (January 6, 1617), quoted in *The Letters of Claudio Monteverdi*, trans. Denis Stevens (Cambridge: Cambridge University Press, 1980), 126.

[25] Letter to Alessandro Striggio (May 22, 1627), quoted in Ibid., 318.

[26] Benedetto Marcello, letter to Jacopo Perti, October 4, 1711, quoted in Piero Weiss, *Letters of Composers*, 62.

[27] Quoted in Claude Palisca, *Baroque Music* (Englewood Cliffs: Prentice Hall, 1981), 236ff.

[28] Agostino Agazzari, "On Playing," 426.

of emotions through music. The great opera librettist, Metastasio, for example, had begun to worry, in a letter of 1747, about the effectiveness of rapidly changing emotions in opera.

> The audience cannot interest themselves, as you would wish, in the agitations of your personages, because there is not sufficient time allowed to render them either hateful or amiable. If the mind of a spectator is removed from its usual temperament and tranquility, the interest does not continue long enough to be remembered in the next scene: so that it becomes torpid and unwilling to be pleased, even to that degree of nausea which soon comes on for those very beauties, which, otherwise, might successfully have solicited and seduced.[29]

In a letter of 1749 to Adolfo Hasse, concerning the opera *Attilio Regolo*, Metastasio reflects the fact that composers were beginning to write out symbols of feelings formerly left to the singers.

> I should hope from such hands as yours, that a recitative always accompanied by instruments, would not be such a tiresome thing as it usually is, from others ... You likewise so well know how to perfect the art, by the judicious and alternate use of *pianos* and *fortes*, by *rinforzandos*, by *staccatos*, *slurs*, accelerating and retarding the measure, *arpeggios*, shakes, *sostenutos* ... [30]

Regarding the music itself, Tosi, in his treatise on singing, stresses in several places that the singer should only sing the *best* music. The best music, he observes, has the capacity to "instruct the student, perfect the skillful, and delight the listener."[31] Tosi had a distinct preference for the slower expressive music of the earlier Baroque opera and thus advises singers to tell composers that they want to sing, not dance.[32]

Tosi's comment that singers should sing and not dance, is a reflection of the fact that Italian opera, particularly in Venice, had become as much an entertainment form as an art form, or as a visitor in 1729 gave its purpose, "to tickle the ears."

[29] Letter to Abate Pasquini, in Charles Burney, *Memoirs of the Life and Writings of the Abate Metastasio* (New York: Da Capo Press, 1971), I, 191.

[30] Letter to Adolfo Hasse, 1749, in Ibid., I, 326

[31] P. F. Tosi, *Observations*, VII, xxiv.

[32] Ibid., VII, xxxiv.

Care has been taken that none of these famous singers should be disfigured with a beard; however, their smooth faces with their shrill and effeminate voice seem to be something out of character, when they make their appearance on the stage like warlike heroes, animating their troops to second their bravery. But we must observe that operas are not calculated to please the judgment, but to tickle the ear; so that propriety of characters is as little to be expected in these pieces, as sublime and poetical language.[33]

Perhaps only because opera had become an entertainment instead of an art, can one understand a comment in a letter of Abate Conti to Madame de Caylus, in 1727, that "Vivaldi has produced three operas in less than three months."[34] Whatever is the truth of that contention, it is clear that Vivaldi had become responsive to the relationship of his operas and the public. In a letter of 1737 he expresses his concern that poor ticket sales would constitute a risk to his reputation.[35]

Ultimately, the responsibility for the communication of emotions in music falls to the performer. If there is still a reader somewhere who is under the impression that baroque music was mechanical and boring, the description of Corelli quoted at the top of this essay should make him wonder if he has been misinformed. Just as this description of Corelli seems very modern to us, so does the prescription for achieving this level of communication offered by the great baroque violinist, Francesco Geminiani.

These extraordinary emotions are indeed most easily excited when accompanied with words; and I would besides advise, as well the composer as the performer, who is ambitions to inspire his audience to be first inspired himself, which he cannot fail to be if he chooses a work of genius, if he makes himself thoroughly acquainted with all its beauties; and if while his imagination is warm and glowing he pours the same exalted spirit into his own performance.[36]

As we have mentioned above, one of the central themes of the Baroque in music was a search for just how music communicates the emotions. Many musicians commented on this, as for example, the great organist, Girolamo Frescobaldi,

[33] J. G. Keysler, *Travels* (London, 1756), III, 262.

[34] Alan Kendall, *Vivaldi* (London: Granada Publishing, 1979), 129.

[35] A. Cavicchi, "Inediti nell' episolario Vivaldi-Bentivoglio," in *Nuova Rivista Musicale Italiana*, I (May/June, 1967), 55ff. In another letter [Ibid., 77], Vivaldi adds, "whoever takes away my honor may take away my life."

[36] Francesco Geminiani, *Treatise of Good Taste*, 4.

who reminds the student that the source of the emotions is found in the music itself.

> Since it also seems that many may have neglected the practice of studying the score, I wished to point out that in these things, which do not seem to be governed by the rules of counterpoint, one must first of all seek the feeling of the passage and the aim of the author concerning the effect on the ear, and the way in which one should try to play them.[37]

Frescobaldi mentions the importance of studying the score again in his *Fiori musicali*, where he suggests this practice separates the "true gold of the *virtuosi* from the actions of the ignorant."[38]

In 1749, Francesco Geminiani also complains that the soul of the expression should lie in the composition itself, not in the additions of the singer.

> What is commonly called good taste in singing and playing, has been thought for some years past to destroy the true melody, and the intention of their composers. It is supposed by many that a real good taste cannot possibly be acquired by any rules of art; it being a peculiar gift of nature, indulged only to those who have naturally a good ear: And as most flatter themselves to have this perfection, hence it happens that he who sings or plays, thinks of nothing so much as to make continually some favorite Passages or Graces,[39] believing that by this means he shall be thought to be a good performer, not perceiving that playing in good taste doth not consist of frequent Passages, but in expressing with strength and delicacy the intention of the composer. This expression is what everyone should endeavor to acquire and it may be easily obtained by any person, who is not too fond of his own opinion.[40]

Marco da Gagliano, in the preface to his *Dafne* (1608), on the other hand, finds feelings in the words.

> The scene of Apollo's lament should be sung with the greatest possible emotion; at the same time the singer should take care to make a crescendo when the words demand it.[41]

Giovanni Bonachelli, in 1642, adds the interesting suggestion that even the tempo is adjusted according to the emotions of the words.

---

[37] Girolamo Frescobaldi, "Capricci fatti sopra diversi soggetti," quoted in MacClintock, *Readings*, 135.

[38] Quoted in Ibid., 136.

[39] Meaning improvisation.

[40] Francesco Geminiani, *A Treatise of Good Taste in the Art of Musick*, 2.

[41] Quoted in Ibid., 192ff.

> First they must be concerted together, and the feeling [*affetti*] of the words and the speed must be observed, and especially in the reciting styles, or representative, as others say, and in accordance with the feeling one must guide the beat, sensing it now fast, now slow, according to the occasion, now liveliness, and now languour, as indeed anyone will easily know immediately who possesses the fine manner of singing.[42]

Tosi, although writing a treatise on vocal technique, was never so passionate as when he spoke of "heart."

> Oh! how great a master is the heart! Confess it, my beloved singers, and gratefully admit, that you would not have arrived at the highest rank of the profession if you had not been its scholars; admit, that in a few lessons from it, you learned the most beautiful expressions, the most refined taste, the most noble action, and the most exquisite graces: Admit (though it be hardly credible) that the heart corrects the defects of nature, since it softens a voice that's harsh, betters an indifferent one, and perfects a good one: Admit, when the heart sings you cannot dissemble, nor has truth a greater power of persuading. And, lastly, do you convince the world that from the heart alone you have learned that *Je ne scai quoy*, that pleasing charm, that so subtly passes from vein to vein, and makes its way to the very soul.[43]

With respect to general Italian literature, the seventeenth century is usually not considered a strong period. One historian, Buckner Trawick, for example, declared, "Italian literature of the seventeenth century hardly deserves to be mentioned."[44] But we cannot pass over the great poet, Marino (1569–1625), who recognized what the musicians were saying, that emotions are the heart of music.

> Music pleases all, but more than all the rest
> delights the restless souls of those in love,
> nor can tormented heart find other peace
> or refuge than in melody and songs.
> 'Tis true indeed that music has the power
> sometimes to call forth doleful sighs and tears,
> and thus it mingles two contrary ends;
> it cheers the cheerful, saddens still the sad.[45]

---

[42] Giovanni Bonachelli, *Corona di sacri gigli a una, due, tre, quattro, e cinque voci* (Venice, 1642), preface.

[43] P. F. Tosi, *Observations*, IX, xliv.

[44] Buckner Trawick, *World Literature* (New York: Barnes & Noble, 1955), II, 33.

[45] Giambattista Marino, *L'Adone* [1623], trans. Harold Priest (Ithaca: Cornell University Press, 1967), VII, 62. Marino (1569–1625) was a genuine court poet, working for a cardinal, a duke, a queen regent and a king of France. As a young man in Naples, Marino abandoned his studies in law to sow a few wild oats. He was jailed several times, for forgery and for the death, during an abortion, of a young girl he had seduced. Escaping from jail in 1600, his life began to have some stability after he moved to Rome.

2
Thoughts on the Beginning of Italian Opera

FIRST OF ALL, opera was a child of Humanism. By Humanism in music we mean the rediscovery of the importance of music as a vehicle for communicating the emotions. The catalyst for the beginning of this movement was the rediscovery of the lost books of the ancient Greek philosophers, the early Church having previously attempted to destroy all copies and then establishing for 1,000 years a ridiculous theory that music was only a branch of mathematics.

When these famous lost books, in particular those by Plato and Aristotle, were rediscovered in Arabic translations during the late Middle Ages, and when gradually translations into European languages were made available, Europeans interested in music focused on the descriptions of performances of music in which the audience was obviously moved by emotions. One of these passages is found in Plato's *Ion*, a discussion between Socrates and Ion, a rhapsodist. The rhapsodist was a performer who, using a style and technique unknown today, but apparently something between singing and speech, gave public performances of memorized poetry, including such works as Homer. The passage reads,

> SOCRATES. Are you not carried out of yourself, and does not your soul in an ecstasy seem to be among the persons or places of which you are speaking ...?[1]

[1] This is always translated as "speaking," but "singing" would be equally accurate, as the style lay in between. In truth, we have no way of knowing how near the performance of the Rhapsodist was to speaking or singing, but the tradition of the lyric poets, which developed out of it, was distinctly *sung* poetry.

> ION. Only too well; for I look down upon them from the stage, and behold the various emotions of pity, wonder, sternness, stamped upon their faces when I am performing.[2]

[2] Plato, *Ion*, 534c–535e.

The Renaissance persons interested in music read such passages, and others such as descriptions of actual performances in Homer, and asked, "How come our music [polyphony] does not do this?"

It seems clear that the academy in Florence in the late sixteenth century, known as the Camerata, which is credited with the development of opera, had this in mind and that their goal was to create a stage production which communicated a more natural emotional life than the current stage productions of spoken dialog. And this is certainly confirmed by the comments of the very first composers and musicians involved in the birth of opera, who all spoke of the communication of emotions being their first goal. We will return to these quotations below, but first we must explain some nonsense about the early opera which the reader will find in music texts and may find confusing.

First, it is important to remember that nearly all poetry until about the fourteenth century was sung. Second, there is no question that several poets of the Renaissance made comments to the effect that the emotions are found in the *words*. This was a very understandable error on their part, based on their lack of our modern clinical understanding. The fact is words have no emotional content at all. Words, as part of a language, have a meaning, which can be found in a dictionary. But a single word of the language, such as "pain," carries no emotion at all. The word only becomes associated with an emotion when an individual's experience is added, either the personal emotional experience of the listener or the individual's oral interpretation based on his emotional experience. Clinically speaking, the experiential side of us, the right hemisphere of the brain, adds emotion to the words when we speak or sing. Since these emotions are genetic and universal, the listener understands, in at least a general sense, the emotion being conveyed. The Renaissance poets, unfortunately, did not observe their sung poetry carefully enough to understand what was really happening. The fact is, when these Renaissance poets said, "the emotions are in the words," what they really meant was, "the emotions are in the manner in which the words are sung."

Nevertheless, the Renaissance poets did say that the emotions are in the words. They, and later historians, found a line by Socrates about sung poetry, quoted in Plato's *Republic*, Book III, which they took not only to support their statement but to demonstrate, as humanists, their perceived link with ancient Greece. The comment by Socrates reads,

> ... for our principle is that rhythm and harmony are regulated by the words, and not the words by them.[3]

[3] Plato's *The Republic* is thought to date from c. 360 BC. The translation we use is by Benjamin Jowett.

This line from Socrates has been frequently and widely quoted and has led to some statements by famous music historians which might potentially be misleading to students. For example, one finds:

Manfred Bukofzer, in his famous book, *Music in the Baroque Era*,

> ... *the word is the master of harmony*.[4]

[4] Manfred F. Bukofzer, *Music in the Baroque Era* (New York: Norton, 1947), 4, quoting Berardi's *Miscellanea Musicale* (1689). The italics are ours.

Julius Portnoy, in discussing "The Aesthetics of Music in the Baroque Era," writes of the style of composition in the first operas (called "recitative," but meaning something different from what we mean by recitative today), that it was created in order that,

> *music could be subordinated to the words*.[5]

[5] Julius Portnoy, *The Philosopher and Music* (New York: The Humanities Press, 1954), 128.

Such conclusions seem to imply that in opera the words are more important than the music. But this is wrong. This has never been true, either now or in the seventeenth century. No one alive has ever gone to an opera performance of Mozart's to hear the words.

Perhaps we should take another look at Socrates' definition, which has always been quoted out of context. First of all, in this discussion of sung poetry by Socrates, it is very clear that he understood the power which music exerted on the listener. He observed here,

> ... musical training is a more potent instrument than any other, because rhythm and harmony find their way into the inward places of the soul.

In this same passage in the *Republic* it is also clear that Socrates understood the power of harmony and that harmony was an emotional key for affecting the behavior of the listener.

> Of the harmonies I know nothing, but I want to have one warlike, to sound the note or accent which a brave man utters in the hour of danger and stern resolve, or when his cause is failing, and he is going to wounds or death or is overtaken by some other evil, and at every such crisis meets the blows of fortune with firm step and a determination to endure; and another to be used by him in times of peace and freedom of action, when there is no pressure of necessity, and he is seeking to persuade God by prayer, or man by instruction and admonition, or on the other hand, when he is expressing his willingness to yield to persuasion or entreaty or admonition, and which represents him when by prudent conduct he has attained his end, not carried away by his success, but acting moderately and wisely under the circumstances, and acquiescing in the event.

In this same discussion we find the belief that rhythm also contributed to the creation of emotion in the listener.

> Then, I said, we must take Damon into our counsels; and he will tell us what rhythms are expressive of meanness, or insolence, or fury, or other unworthiness, and what are to be reserved for the expression of opposite feelings.

It is in the above context, the importance of harmony and rhythm for underlying emotion in sung poetry, that we come to the famous line of Socrates, which reads in full,

> And also that good and bad rhythm naturally assimilate to a good and bad style; and that harmony and discord in like manner follow style; for our principle is that rhythm and harmony are regulated by the words, and not the words by them.

We hope the reader can see that Socrates' *real* meaning in this discussion of *sung* poetry was that harmony and rhythm must be in correspondence with the emotions of the words of the poetry. He clearly did not have in mind the interpretation that the words were *more important* than music.

The reader may find it curious that in this entire discussion by Socrates he never uses the word, "melody." But this is only because in a time when almost all poetry was *sung*, the "words" and "melody" were *synonymous*. Ironically, modern clinical research, not to mention common experience, prove that it is melody, and not so much harmony or rhythm, which communicates emotions in music.

One of the creators of the earliest opera got it right and did give melody its correct importance. Monteverdi, in a letter of 1633, proposes to write a book on the subject of the new Baroque style versus the old Renaissance polyphonic style.

> I am dividing the book into three parts corresponding to the three aspects of *Melody*. In the first I discuss word-setting, in the second, harmony, and in the third, the rhythmic part.[6]

In the Foreword of *Il quinto libro*, written by his brother, Monteverdi makes this point perfectly clear: *Melody* is the most important element and it is to melody (with words) that *harmony is the servant*.

> This my brother [Monteverdi] will make apparent, knowing for certain that in a kind of composition such as this of his, *music turns on the perfection of the melody*, considered *from which point of view* the harmony, from being the mistress [as it was in polyphony], becomes the servant of the words, and the words [with melody] the mistress of the harmony, to which way of thinking the Second Practice, or modern usage, tends.[7]

In case this is not clear enough, Monteverdi is even more explicit in the passage which follows.

> By First Practice [sixteenth century polyphony] he understands the [Practice] that considers the harmony not commanded, but commanding, not the servant, but the mistress of the words ...
>
> By Second Practice ... he understands the [Practice] *that turns on the perfection of the melody*, that is, the one that

[6] Letter to Giovanni Doni (October 22, 1633), quoted in *The Letters of Claudio Monteverdi,* trans. Denis Stevens (Cambridge: Cambridge University Press, 1980), 410. The italics are ours.

[7] Oliver Strunk, *Source Readings in Music History* (New York: Norton, 1950), 407ff.

considers harmony not commanding, but commanded, and makes the words [including melody] the mistress of the harmony.

Monteverdi concludes this passage by quoting Plato once again as saying, "Does not music also turn on the perfection of the melody?"[8] Monteverdi's perspective was that it is the *melody with words* which is the mistress and that the remaining elements of harmony and rhythm are the servant to these. He does *not* say music is the servant of the words. Indeed, the title which he says he will use for his projected new book was to be, *Melody, or the Second Musical Practice*. Nothing could more clearly indicate that the emphasis was melody and not words.

We believe that Monteverdi here must surely have been reflecting the basic idea of his fellow musicians who created the first opera. Surely their idea was to create a performance vehicle which communicated stronger emotions than mere spoken drama as they knew it. This seems clear in their own statements. Cavalieri, in the preface to his *La rappresentatione di Anima* (1600) says his goal is to "move listeners to different emotions, such as pity and joy, tears and laughter."[9] Caccini, in his *Le Nuove Musiche*, writes that the goal was "to move the emotions of the soul."[10]

The basic question of the Camerata was, "*how* do you make music correspond with the words?" Their answer was to begin by making the music correspond rhythmically with the style of spoken Italian. This was made very clear by one of the most important members of the Camerata, Giovani Bardi (1534–1612):

> Music is nothing else than the art and fashion of giving to words their proper time-value; since they should be *sung* either fast or slow, accordingly as they are short or long; and practical music is an arrangement of the words (which have been set by the poet into verses of various measure, according to their long or short syllables) such that the words, *sung by the human voice,* shall move, now fast, now slow, now in high tones, now in low, the *song* being either entrusted to *the voice* alone, or accompanied by instruments. *This is Plato's definition,* with which Aristotle and other learned men agree.[11]

[8] Plato, *Gorgias,* 449D.

[9] Quoted in Nino Pirrotta and Elena Povoledo, *Music and Theatre from Poliziano to Monteverdi* (Cambridge: Cambridge University Press, 1982), 241.

[10] *Le Nuove Musiche,* 45.

[11] Quoted in Donald N. Ferguson, *A History of Musical Thought* (New York: Appleton-Century-Crofts, 1948), 243.

This is corroborated by a letter of 1587 by Bardi to Caccini, another of the founders of opera. Speaking of the same passage by Socrates in Plato, Bardi says the sum of the elements mentioned here, which Bardi gives as speech, harmony and rhythm, is "words well *sung*" [*parole ben cantate*].[12]

[12] Quoted in Claude Palisca, *The Florentine Camerata* (New Haven: Yale University Press, 1989), 92ff.

And this is exactly what they did in the first operas. They have left a kind of rhythmic-melodic sketch in notation, leaving to the singers the duty of adding the emotions through their style of singing and especially through improvisation, a subject to which one of the founders of opera, Caccini, devoted an entire book. And, of course, improvisation continued to be a fundamental part of opera until the twentieth century.

Let us remember, that is exactly what we all do everyday in speaking. And let us also remember that in the performance of music we have no other choice, for the Church has left us with a notation system of their invention which to this very day is utterly and completely devoid of any symbols representing emotions. One *can* say that to sing these first operas today on the basis of only what is on paper makes no sense whatsoever to the listener.

In any case, the potential importance of this new medium appears to have been understood at once for several participants immediately put forth claims for the credit of the birth.[13] Caccini insisted on replacing some of the music of Peri's *Euridice* with his own compositions under the argument that the singers who were his students could sing only music written by their master, and then tried to claim ownership of the work itself. And when Rinuccini printed his libretto for *Euridice* still another composer, Cavalieri, writes in a letter of November 1600, "Rinuccini acts ... as if he had been the inventor of this way of representing [action] in music; but this was invented by me, and everyone knows this."

[13] This is discussed in Pirrotta and Povoledo, *Music and Theatre*, 238ff.

Everyone knows of the rapid expansion from Florence to Rome and to Venice, and from there throughout Europe, and of the fact that Italian opera planted the seeds which would create the Classical Period style. What is little mentioned in music history texts is the fact that this wonderful new idea, a medium recreating the most noble ideals of ancient Greece with its emphasis on emotional expression, very soon disintegrated into a shameless entertainment medium. It required the efforts of Gluck and Mozart to make opera an art form again. The same thing happened soon after Mozart's death, when Paris returned the opera to an entertainment form. Once again an artist came forward to attempt to make it an art form, who was of course, Wagner.

During the course of the seventeenth century opera replaced the older Renaissance allegorical pageants and horse shows as the entertainment of preference. It is no surprise that much of the old pageantry remained, as we can see in a description of a performance of the opera *Berenice* (1680), by Giovanni Freschi, which included a procession of a chorus of 100 virgins, a hoard of soldiers, 2 elephants, 6 trumpeters on horse, 6 drummers, 6 trombones, 6 "great" flutes, 6 minstrels with Turkish instruments, 6 with "octave" flutes and 6 "cymbalists."[14] And like the earlier allegorical pageants, the seventeenth century operas did not fail to underwrite the themes of power and privilege which kept the nobles comfortable and the lower class at bay.

Venice made opera available to the public and alone had seven different theaters for opera by the end of the seventeenth century and between 1662 and 1680 nearly 100 different operas were heard there.[15] There is an interesting contemporary account of opera in Venice, written by a canon of St. Mark's, Cristoforo Ivanovich, in 1681.[16] He begins by describing the various entertainments to be enjoyed in Venice, season by season. It is under Winter, that he turns to opera.

> This brings the Carnival season, for which outsiders flock to the city, and which sees the citizens themselves in continuous activity, after the year's employment in political or domestic affairs. The opera houses are first to begin; this they do with incredible magnificence and splendor, by no means inferior to that practiced in various places by the magnificence of princes, with the sole difference that the latter procure the enjoyment of all through their own generosity, while opera in Venice is business and thus lacks that decorum with which marriages

[14] John Sainsbury, *Dictionary of Musicians* (London, 1825).

[15] A comprehensive description of opera in Venice is given in Lorenzo Bianconi, *Music in the Seventeenth Century*, trans. David Bryant (Cambridge: Cambridge University Press, 1987), 180ff.

[16] Quoted in Ibid., 303ff.

and births are frequently celebrated by princes with a view to the greater display of their magnificence and power. The performance of these *drammi,* as also of comedies, continues without interruption until the final day of Carnival; in this way, each evening brings a variety of entertainments of several hours' length, held in a number of different theaters (each of which traditionally offers two different productions per season as a means of drawing the crowds).

He compares the construction of modern theaters with those of ancient Rome, pointing out that instead of tiers there are now private boxes. In the middle section, however, "benches are rented out on a day-to-day basis without social distinction." Whereas the entertainments of ancient Rome were famously brutal, today, he observes,

> musical theater exists more as relief for the soul and as virtuous recreation. The appearance of ingenious machines, as suggested by the drama, combines with the costumes and scenic display in a way which proves extremely attractive and which fully satisfies the universal curiosity aroused. In this way, lifelike elephants and real-life camels have been seen to walk the stage, as also grandiose chariots drawn by horses or other wild beasts; other sights include flying horses, dancing horses, the most magnificent machines represented by air, earth and sea with fantastic contrivances and laudable invention, to the point at which royal apartments, illuminated as for night, have been seen to descend from the air with the entire company of actors and instrumentalists, and then to return whence they came, with the great admiration of all.

The canon discusses various arrangements by which one can pay for the private boxes, but in general he is alarmed at the great cost of opera.

> A theater, before enjoying any profit whatever, has many expenses to sustain, all of which regard the performance of the dramas. The first and greatest of these expenses concerns the remuneration of the singers, the pretensions of these men and women having reached excessive levels (where earlier they were happy to perform irrespective of gain, or at most for honest recognition). It is also necessary to pay the composer of the *dramma per musica.* There follow the expenses for the costumes, *mutazioni di scena* and construction of the machines;

an agreement must be reached with the *maestro de' balli,* and the various instrumentalists and theatrical hands must be paid on a nightly basis ... Sufficient, at the beginning, were two delightful voices with a few arias to bring pleasure and a limited number of *mutazioni di scena* to satisfy the curiosity; today, more attention is paid to a voice that does not live up to expectations than to many of the greatest singers in Europe ... These are the reasons for which expenses increase year by year, though prices at the door have actually fallen. The very continuation of opera could well be placed in jeopardy if this current state of affairs is not regulated more carefully.

He concludes with a summary of the kinds of profit which opera brings to a town, including financial profit. More important than this, he finds,

No pleasure can be greater than that which is born from the harmonies taught by the very motion of the spheres: these qualities, together with the other particular circumstances of theatrical entertainments, render the latter enjoyable thrice over: pomp and display for the eye, music for the ear, poetry for the intellect.

Being a prince of the Church, and thus associated with the noble class, he has one more worry:

The low price charged at the entrance reduces the means available to meet the considerable cost of the pomp and display, facilitates access on the part of the ignorant and tumultuous masses and lowers the dignity of that very virtue which exists no less for delight than for profit.

One visiting diplomat was amazed to find performances of opera continuing in Venice even in times of war.[17] The Englishman, John Evelyn, documents well established opera in Venice already when he visited in 1645.

[17] He is quoted in Ellen Rosand, "Venice, 1580–1680," *The Early Baroque Era* (Englewood Cliffs: Prentice Hall, 1994), 90.

This night, having with my Lord Bruce taken our places before, we went to the Opera, where comedies and other plays are represented in recitative music, by the most excellent musicians, vocal and instrumental, with variety of scenes painted and contrived with no less art of perspective, and machines for flying in the air, and other wonderful nations; taken together, it is one of the most magnificent and expensive diversions the wit of man can invent. The history was, Hercules in Lydia; the scenes changed thirteen times. The famous voices, Anna Rencia, a Roman, and reputed the best treble of women; but there was an eunuch who, in my opinion, surpassed her.[18]

[18] John Evelyn, *Diary* (London, 1907), I, 202.

By the end of the century, a French visitor in Venice was relatively unimpressed.

It is an undeniable matter of fact that the ornaments of those here fall extremely short of [Parisian operas]: the habits are poor, no dances, and commonly no machines, nor any illuminations, only some candles here and there, which deserve not to be mentioned. It is dangerous not to magnify the Italian music, or to say, at least, anything against it.[19]

[19] F. M. Misson, *A New Voyage to Italy* (London, 1695), I, 191ff.

Joseph Addison, visiting in 1701, was more impressed with opera in Venice, although he found it somewhat ridiculous "to hear one of the rough old Romans squeaking through the mouth of a eunuch."[20]

But this was also public opera and some of the eyewitness accounts of the behavior of the public are quite remarkable. The visiting German, Uffenbach, refers to an opera performance in 1715 which Vivaldi conducted:

[20] Joseph Addison, *Remarks on Several Parts of Italy in 1701* (London, 1705), 96ff.

For fear of being maltreated and covered with spit as on the previous occasion, we took a box, not very expensive, and we had our revenge in behaving in relation to the people below as people had to us, a thing which previously would have seemed impossible to me ... The singers were incomparable.[21]

[21] Quoted in Kendall, *Vivaldi* (London: Granada Publishing, 1979), 97.

Curiously, similar behavior is mentioned five years later by a visiting Englishman.

There are no open galleries, as in London, but the whole from bottom to top is all divided into boxes, which one with another will contain about six persons each. They have a scandalous custom [in Venice] of spitting out of the upper boxes, as well as throwing parings of apples or oranges, upon the company in the pit, which they do at random, without any regard where it falls; though it sometimes happens upon some of the best quality; who, though they have boxes of their own, will often come into the pit, either for the better seeing of the company, or sometimes to be nearer the stage, for the better hearing of some favorite songs.[22]

[22] Ibid., 110.

This same visitor also mentions that some listeners bring their own copies of the libretti, which they read with the help of "wax candles in their hands." The candles, unfortunately, "are frequently put out by the [spit] from above."

Although the noble aspirations of the Camerata had long since given way to the demands of entertainment, Italian opera, as it spread across Europe, was a source of pride to Italians, as we can see in this rather smug observation by Pier Jacopo Martello.

> Music alone ... contains the all important secrets of the separation of the soul from all human concerns, at least for that period of time in which the soul is held enthralled by the notes in their artful handling of the consonance of voices and instruments ... This art has been developed to the utmost perfection in Italy; it is thus only correct that Italy should adopt it as its favorite and most magnificent type of theatrical entertainment, one indeed which raises a smile even in the most severe of judges; likewise, it is only correct that foreign nations should consent to the importation of a model of entertainment so justly found pleasing in Italy.[23]

[23] Pier Jacopo Martello, *Storia e ragione d'ogni poesia* (1744), quoted in Bianconi, *Music in the Seventeenth Century*, 167.

Italian opera, as it spread throughout Europe, carried with it the first celebrity singers, who became the daily topic of discussion in newspapers and by the public. We will allow sketches of two sopranos from Venice represent this large body of colorful singers.

Francesca Cuzzoni (1700–1770) made her debut in Venice in 1718 and her success was followed by performances throughout Italy. She was known for her perfect intonation, creativity in improvisation and by a unique ability to crescendo and diminuendo by minute degrees.

She made her first of many trips to London in 1722 where she was engaged by Handel, who greeted her by announcing, "Madame, I well know that you are a veritable female devil; but I myself, I will have you know, am Bellzebub, chief of the devils." In a rehearsal for her appearance in his *Ottone*, she declared that she disliked the aria, "Falsa immagine," and refused to sing it. She quickly changed her mind when Handel threatened to throw her out a window and thereafter this aria became the one that made her career in London. She is well remembered for her musical duels with another Italian soprano in London, Bordoni.

Faustina Bordoni (1700–1781) was born to a noble Italian family, one which previously governed the Venetian Republic. Famous for what Charles Burney called "a new kind of singing, by running improvisation with a neatness and velocity which astonished all who heard her," she was heard by Handel, who took her to London for a production of his *Alessandro* in 1726.

The London audience, however, quickly took sides, some becoming supporters of Bordoni and some of Cuzzoni, and began to compete in the applause and boos they awarded their favorite. During a performance of Bononcini's *Astianatte*, in 1727, when Bordoni tried to sing the supporters of Cuzzoni rose up in a chorus of hisses, boos, and roars. A fight broke out in the pit and soon, on the stage itself, the two sopranos began to fight and tear each other's hair while the spectators smashed the scenery! This great competition was satirized by Gay in his *The Beggar's Opera* of 1728.[24]

The great popularity of the *prima donna* with the general audience cannot be entirely separated from the fact that opera itself was by the end of the Baroque becoming more and more of an entertainment form. The great librettist, Metastasio, expresses his concern for the direction of Italian opera in a letter of 1750.

> In Italy, at present, there is a taste for nothing but extravagance, and vocal symphonies; in which we sometimes hear an excellent violin, flute or oboe; but never the singing of a human creature. So that music is now to excite no other emotion than that of surprise. Things are carried to such excess, that if not soon reformed, we shall justly become the buffoons of all other nations. Composers and performers being only ambitious of tickling the ear, without ever thinking of the hearts of the audience, are generally condemned in all theaters, to the disgraceful office of degrading the acts of an opera, into

[24] Bordini married the famous German composer Johann Adolf Hasse and followed him to Dresden where they lived in happiness for thirty years, before retiring to Venice. Cuzzoni, passing through the Netherlands after she had lost her voice, was thrown into prison for her debts. By giving performances for the governor of the prison, she gradually repaid her debt and made her way to Bologna. There, in extreme poverty and squalor, she supported herself by making buttons.

intermezzi for the dances, which occupy the attention of the people, and chief part of the spectators.[25]

Metastasio was all the more sensitive to this decay in the aesthetic aim of opera for he had been witness to an earlier period in which audiences wept in response to the singing on the stage.[26]

[25] Letter to Farinelli, August 1, 1750, in Charles Burney, *Memoirs of the Life and Writings of the Abate Metastasio* (New York: Da Capo Press, 1971), I, 375ff.

[26] Letter of 1731, in Ibid., 75.

3
Italian Views on Baroque Performance Practice

FROM THE NEW EMPHASIS ON FEELING in performance at the beginning of the seventeenth century it followed that there was a new respect for the purpose of rehearsal. In a letter of 1607, Monteverdi explains that he is sending the music to a singer in advance,

> so that he can rehearse it and get a firm grasp of the melody together with the other gentlemen singers, because it is very difficult for a singer to perform a part which he has not first practiced, and greatly damaging to the composition itself, as it is not completely understood on being sung for the first time.[1]

A letter of 1620 gives some indication of what he meant by sufficient rehearsal.

> Now consider, Your Lordship: what do you think can be done when more than four hundred lines, which have to be set to music are still lacking? I can envisage no other result than bad singing of the poetry, bad playing of the instruments, and bad musical ensemble. These are not things to be done hastily, as it were; and you know from *Arianna* that after it was finished and learned by heart, [then!] five months of strenuous rehearsal took place.[2]

If for no other reason, the context of the rehearsal must have changed dramatically due to the new sense of freedom in time, something which followed naturally from the emphasis on feeling and something impossible under the

[1] Letter to Annibale Iberti (July 28, 1607), quoted in *The Letters of Claudio Monteverdi*, trans. Denis Stevens (Cambridge: Cambridge University Press, 1980), 51.

[2] Letter to Alessandro Striggio (January 9, 1620), quoted in Ibid., 160.

rigid proportional time system of the old polyphonic style. Already in 1615, in a letter of Monteverdi, we find a new criteria for tempo. In sending the music for a court ballet, he cautions that the works must be conducted "with a beat suitable to the character of the melodies."[3] In the same year Frescobaldi (1583–1643) was even more explicit in associating both tempo and rubato with the expression of the text.

[3] Letter to Annibale Iberti (November 21, 1615), quoted in Ibid., 108.

> I well know how performers like to indulge in impressive ornaments and many passages. Therefore I take the liberty of adding the following observations to these, my modest products, which I herewith publish ...
>
> These pieces should not be played to a strict beat any more than modern madrigals which, though difficult, are made easier by taking the beat now slower, now faster, and by even pausing altogether in accordance with the expression and meaning of the text.[4]

[4] Girolamo Frescobaldi, *Toccatas and Partitas*, Book I (1615), quoted in Morgenstern, *Composers on Music*, 24.

By the end of the Baroque Period, the famous singing teacher, Tosi, was becoming alarmed on hearing singers alter the tempo solely for the reason of engaging in virtuoso improvisation.

> Even among the professors of the first rank there are few, but what are almost insensibly deceived into an irregularity, or hastening of time, and often of both ...
>
> I do not advise a student to imitate several of the Moderns in their manner of singing arias, it is from their neglect of keeping time, which ought to be inviolable, and not sacrificed to their beloved [ornamentation].[5]

[5] P. F. Tosi, *Observations on the Florid Song* (London: Wilcox, 1743), VII, xviiff.

One of Tosi's chief objections to the singer delaying time to improvise was that at that moment, since the accompaniment stops, there is suddenly an absence of harmony.

On the other hand, lesser disruptions of tempo, which we call today rubato (Italian: stolen time), were not only permitted by Tosi, but were considered as a characteristic of good taste.

> Whoever does not know how to steal time in singing ... is destitute of the best taste and greatest knowledge.
>
> The stealing of time, in the [adagio] is an honorable theft in one that sings better than others, provided he makes a restitution with ingenuity.[6]

[6] Ibid., IX, xliff.

> ......
> [A singer] wants that which teaches to anticipate the time, knowing where to lose it again; and, which is still more charming, to know how to lose it, in order to recover it again.[7]

[7] Ibid., IX, lxiii.

We also see in a comment by Tosi a reflection of an earlier use of the Italian terms to reflect style, rather than just tempo as familiar to us today. He recommends one should imitate the *Cantabile* of the [early Baroque singers] and the *Allegro* of the moderns.[8]

[8] Ibid., VI, xxi.

While it is our belief that dynamic variety has always existed in performance, the appearance of the music to the eye notwithstanding, one nevertheless senses a new enthusiasm in the discussion of this topic. Scipione Maffei, for example, observed in 1711,

> It is common knowledge among lovers of music that one of the chief methods by which the expert in that art contrive the secret of bringing particular delight to their listeners, is the piano and forte in subject and answer, or the gradual diminishing of the sound little by little, and the sudden return to the full volume of the instrument; which recourse is used frequently and with wonderful effect, in the great concerts of Rome.[9]

[9] Scipione Maffei, "Nuova Invenzione d'un Gravecembalo," in *Giornale dei Letterati d'Italia* (Venice, 1711), V, 144.

Fantini, in 1638, mentions one of the dynamic effects most common to the period.

> It must be pointed out that wherever notes of one, two, or of four beats' length are found, they should be held in a singing fashion, by starting softly, making a crescendo until the middle of the note, and making a diminuendo on the second half until the end of the beat, so that it may hardly be heard.[10]

[10] Quoted in Alan Lumsden, "Woodwind and Brass," in *Performance Practice: Music after 1600* (New York: Norton, 1989), 83.

On the Manners of Singers

It must have been difficult for a singer to please Tosi, even with respect to stage appearance. In general his concern seemed to be that the singer not distract the listener's attention from the music. First, he clearly objected to a cold demeanor on stage.

> From the cold indifference perceived in many singers, one would believe that the science of music implored their favor, to be received by them as their most humble servant.[11]

[11] P. F. Tosi, *Observations*, IX, ii.

But, on the other hand, too much emphasis on stage appearance was also a source of objection.

> Singers who have nothing but outward appearance, pay a debt to the eyes which it owes to the ears.[12]

[12] Ibid., IX, lviii.

Tosi was attentive to the demeanor of his students in every respect, including their personal associations.

> Let the singer shun low and disreputable company, but, above all, such as abandon themselves to scandalous liberties. [Avoid teachers, who] though excellent in this art, whose behavior is vulgar.[13]

[13] Ibid., IX, viiiff.

No doubt every teacher coached his students on the fine points of court etiquette. An interesting passage in Tosi concerns the problem of dealing with a request to sing for free.

> A discreet person will never use such affected expressions as "I cannot sing today—I have a cold . . ." I admit, on certain conjunctures, the pretext is not only suitable, but even necessary; for, to speak the truth, the indiscreet parsimony of some, who would hear music for thanks only, goes so far, that they think a master is immediately obliged to obey them *gratis,* and that the refusal is an offense that deserves resentment and revenge. But if it is a law human and divine, that everybody should live by their honest labor, what barbarous custom obliges a musician to serve without a recompense? A cursed over-bearing; O sordid avarice!
>   A singer, who knows the world, distinguishes between the different manners of commanding; he knows how to refuse without disobliging, and how to obey with a good grace; not being ignorant, that one, who has his interest most at heart, sometimes finds his account in serving without a gratification.[14]

[14] Ibid., IX, xivff.

Included in the broad range of advice which Tosi offered the singer were some more personal admonitions. For one, he reminds the singer of the basis for his status.

If the words are not heard so as to be understood, there will be no great difference between a human voice and an oboe. This defect, although one of the greatest, is today more than common, to the greatest disgrace of the teachers and the profession; and yet they ought to know, that it is only the words which give preference to a singer above an instrumental performer, assuming they were equal in judgment and knowledge.[15]

[15] Ibid., IV, xx.

Tosi also offered the singer this timeless advice:

Whoever does not aspire to the first rank, begins already to give up the second, and little by little will be content with the lowest.[16]

[16] Ibid., VI, xxiv.

We are confident that Tosi is thinking here of artistic heights, and not heights of popularity. He once observed, "a student must not hope for applause, if he has not an utter abhorrence of ignorance."[17] In similar comments he states,

[17] Ibid., VI, xxiii.

It is a folly in a singer to grow vain at the first applause, without reflecting whether they are given by chance, or out of flattery; and if he thinks he deserves them, there is the end of him.[18]

[18] Ibid., IX, xxii.

......
Ignorance hates all that is excellent.[19]

[19] Ibid., VII, 122.

Finally, Tosi makes a nice reflection on critics.

Great advantage may be gained from the ill-natured critics; for, the more intent they are to discover defects, the greater benefit may be received from them without any obligation.[20]

[20] Ibid., IX, xxvi.

On Improvisation

Modern writers distinguish between "ornaments," which refer to the addition by the performer of single, specific ornaments, and "ornamentation," which is really improvisation. The most obvious conclusion that is obtained from Baroque treatises is that improvisation was not only permitted, but expected. Tosi, for example, says a singer may have great knowledge, be able to read at sight the most difficult works and have a well-trained voice which he uses artistically, but if he cannot improvise he cannot be considered distinguished.[21] He adds the important observation that this is a special characteristic of music, for in no other art, such as painting or sculpture, is the artist required to improvise in public. Another way of looking at this responsibility, he points out, is the fact that,

> Poets, painters, sculptors, and even composers, before they expose their works to the public, have all the time needed to correct and polish them; but the singer that commits an error has no remedy; for the fault is committed, and past correction.[22]

For Tosi, the obligation to improvise was nowhere more expected, even required, than in the da capo aria. In one of his most often quoted lines, after explaining the basic form of the aria, Tosi observes that "in repeating the Aria, he that does not vary it for the better, is no great Master."[23] He adds that a moderate singer with good improvisation gets more esteem than a better singer who does not employ it. Indeed, the reason for varied improvisation on the da capo, in Tosi's view, had much to do with judging singers.

> Without varying the Aria, the knowledge of the singers could never be discovered; but from the nature and quality of the variations, it will be easily discerned in two of the greatest singers which is the best.

This famous teacher saw that the singer's success was a matter of experience and taste, not conceptual study alone.

> A singer is under the greatest obligation to the study of the arias; for by them he gains or loses his reputation. To the acquiring this valuable art a few verbal lessons cannot suffice; nor would it be of any great profit to the student, to have a great number of arias, in which a thousand of the most exquisite passages of different sorts were written down: For they would not serve for all purposes, and there would always be lacking that spirit which accompanies extempore performances, and is preferable to all servile imitations.[24]

In general, even taste and skill are of small advantage, he observes, "if one is not ready at extempore embellishments."

---

[21] Ibid., Introduction, vi. When Vivaldi was writing out the figured bass for his violin concerto, RV 340, he got bored and wrote *"per i coglioni,"* "for the dimwits." See Alan Kendall, *Vivaldi* (London: Granada Publishing, 1979), 101.

[22] Ibid., Introduction, vii.

[23] Ibid., VII, ivff.

[24] Ibid., VII, iii.

He only warns that "a superfluity of them should prejudice the composition and confound the ear." But, so much was ornamentation considered part of the performer's art that Tosi could observe that if the student learns well to use appoggiaturas he will be able to,

> laugh at those composers who write them in the music, with the intention either to show they are modern or to show that they understand the art of singing better than the singers.[25]

[25] Ibid., II, xvi.

Improvisation was also anticipated by members of an accompanying ensemble. For Agazzari, writing on the art of the continuo bass in 1607, the principal concern centered only in not covering the solo voice.

> As far as possible try to keep off the same note which the Soprano sings, and avoid making florid divisions on it, so as not to reduplicate the voice part and cover the quality of that voice or the florid divisions which a good singer is making up there.[26]

[26] Agostino Agazzari, "Del sonare sopra' l basso" (Siena, 1607), quoted in Robert Donnington, *The Interpretation of Early Music* (New York, 1964), 171.

Later he also cautions the players of the orchestra to take turn in their ornamentation, for,

> each must regard the other, giving it room and not conflicting with it; if there are many, they must each await their turn and not, chirping all at once like sparrows, try to shout one another down.[27]

[27] Agostino Agazzari, quoted in Oliver Strunk, *Source Readings in Music History* (New York: Norton, 1950), 429.

Particularly interesting insights into ensemble ornamentation is found in a passage written by Pietro della Valle. It is rather amazing to consider this ensemble skill of 1640 when compared to the ensemble experience today. It is especially important for the reader to remember that stylistically everything discussed here was completely absent from the page itself.

> Playing in the company of other instruments does not require the artifices of counterpoint so much as the graces of art; for if the player is good, he does not have to insist so much upon making a display of his own art as upon accommodating himself to all the others ... Those who sing and play well have to give time to one another in company, and they have

to sport with gracefulness of imitations rather than with too
subtle artifices of counterpoints. They will show their art
in knowing how to repeat well and promptly what another
player has done before; and in then giving room to the others
and fit opportunity for them to repeat what they have done;
and in this way, with a varied and no less artful manner,
though neither so difficult nor such deep knowledge, they
will make known to the others their own worth. This is done
nowadays not only by the most excellent, but also by the
ordinary players, and they know how to do it so well that
I do not know how it could have been done better by those
of the past, whom I have not heard. When one plays in the
company of voices, the same thing I said about playing with
instruments must take place, and much more so: because
instruments when serving voices as it were the leaders in
music, must have no other aim than to accompany them
well.[28]

[28] Pietro della Valle, "Della musica dell'età" [1640], quoted in Robert Donnington, *The Interpretation of Early Music* (New York, 1964), 607.

Other writers make an exception to the expectation of improvisation in church music. Viadana, in the preface to his *Church Concerti* of 1602, seems to want to restrict ornamentation to those which he has written out. His suggestion that such improvisation is no longer in style in 1602 must be taken as one of a number of similar clues that sixteenth century polyphony included much more improvisation than the impression given by most historians today.

I have not failed to introduce, where appropriate, certain
figures and cadences, and other convenient opportunities for
ornaments and passagework and for giving other proofs of
the aptitude and elegant style of the singers, although, for the
most part, to facilitate matters, the stock passages have been
used, such as nature itself provides, but more florid . . .

Concerti of this kind must be sung with refinement, discretion, and elegance, using accents with reason and embellishments with moderation and in their proper place: above all, not adding anything beyond what is printed in them, inasmuch as there are sometimes certain singers, who, because they are favored by nature with a certain agility of the throat, never sing the songs as they are written, not realizing that nowadays their like are not acceptable, but are, on the contrary, held in very low esteem indeed, particularly in Rome, where the true school of good singing flourishes.[29]

[29] Lodovico Grossi da Viadana, "Cento concerti ecclesiastici," Preface, quoted in Strunk, *Source Readings*, 420. Viadana (1564–1627) worked as choirmaster in several major cities in Italy and was highly regarded by Praetorius as an authority of the church concerti style.

This was perhaps the exception which Tosi also had in mind, with respect to ensemble improvisation.

> All compositions for more than one voice ought to be sung strictly as they are written; they require no other art than a noble simplicity.[30]

[30] P. F. Tosi, *Observations*, IX, xxv.

With this background, we move on to the more interesting question: What can we deduce regarding the actual style and aesthetic goals in Baroque improvisation?

Giovanni Doni writing in 1635 found that more florid improvisation was being done in the theater, before an audience where "the ignorant always are in greater number than the intelligent." In contrast,

> In chambers, where somewhat delicate music is accustomed to be sung, and in gatherings of people who understand music, the [improvisation] is not required to be used abundantly, but more sparingly.[31]

[31] Giovanni Battista Doni, "Trattati di musica" [1635] quoted in Robert Donnington, *The Interpretation of Early Music*, 180.

Even while observing that improvisation is perhaps more appropriate to the theater, where the audience is "ignorant," Doni still emphasizes the importance of emotional expression in improvisation.

> It is indeed true that improvisation which unfold its passage work [*spasseggiano*] little by little, and uses quicker notes, are more graceful than uniform ones; but perhaps they are not so well suited to sad and languid matters as those which, on the contrary, start quickly, and very gently relax their pace; because they express better a certain languor, and lack of strength. But those which go like waves, that is, now they slacken and now they move on, yet not by jerks and at one blow, but gracefully, are the most beautiful and versatile.[32]

[32] Giovanni Battista Doni, *Trattati di musica* [1635], ed. A. F. Gori (Florence, 1763), II, 69ff.

On the other hand, as another writer confirms, there must have been many singers who gave little thought to the musicality of their ornamentation.

> Many persons are deceived, for they wear themselves out making *gruppi, trilli, passaggi,* and *exclamazioni* with no regard for their purpose or whether or not they are apropos. I certainly do not intend to deprive myself of these adornments,

but I want them to be used in the right time and place...
But where the sense does not demand it, leave aside every ornament, so as not to act like that painter who knew how to paint cypress trees and therefore painted them everywhere.[33]

How, then, does one go about learning this art? Less experienced players, as a treatise of 1608 suggests, wrote out their ornamentation at home ["at his ease"]. The expectation was no doubt the same as one often hears regarding the cadenzas, that it is all right to write them out—so long as they don't sound written out.

> The good and perfect player of the cornett must have a good knowledge of the art of counterpoint, so that he can make up varied passages at his ease, still more extemporaneously...[34]

Judging by comments by Tosi, one expectation was that all ornamentation should be original and not copied from others.

> A singer should not copy... to copy is the part of a scholar, that of a master [performer] is to invent.[35]
> ......
> The most admired graces of a professor ought only to be imitated and not copied; on condition also, that it does not bear even so much as a shadow of resemblance of the original; otherwise, instead of a beautiful imitation, it will become a despicable copy.[36]

The most difficult thing, Tosi says, is to seek inventions which are easy and natural, as well as beautiful.[37] A few of his views on the beautiful in ornamentation include,

> [Ornamentation] must be produced by singular and beautiful invention, remote from all that is vulgar and common...[38]
> [Ornamentation] must be easy in appearance, thereby to give universal delight. That in effect they be difficult that thereby the art of the inventor be the more admired...
> That they be properly introduced, for in the wrong place, they disgust...
> That they should proceed rather from the heart than from the voice, in order to make their way to the heart more easily...
> That they be stolen on the time, to captivate the soul.

[33] Marco da Gagliano, "Dafne," 1608, preface, quoted in Carol MacClintock, *Readings in the History of Music in Performance* (Bloomington: Indiana University Press, 1979), 188. Gagliano (1575–1642) was a prolific composer and writer on music.

[34] Scipione Cerreto, "Dell'arbore musicale" (Naples, 1608), 41, quoted in Donnington, *The Interpretation of Early Music*, 172.

[35] P. F. Tosi, *Observations*, IX, xxxii.

[36] Ibid., IX, xxxviii.

[37] Ibid., VII, xiii.

[38] Ibid., X, vff.

In general, he finds,

> A deficiency of ornaments displeases as much as the too great abundance of them; that a singer makes one languid and dull with too little, and cloys one with too much.[39]

[39] Ibid., IX, lii.

There is one comment by Tosi which leaves us wanting much more detail. What kind of expressive music did he consider was sacred from all ornamentation?

> Where passion speaks, all trills, divisions and graces ought to be silent, leaving it to the sole force of a beautiful expression to persuade.[40]

[40] Ibid., V, iv.

One finds the spirit of many of these views given in a humorous vein by Marcello in his satire on opera, *Theater in the Modern Style,* of 1720. Here, he first recommends that in coaching the singer, the conductor should,

> teach her to enunciate badly, and with this object to teach her a great number of divisions and graces, so that not a single word will be understood, and by this means the music will stand out better and be appreciated.[41]

[41] Benedetto Marcello, "Il treatro alla moda," quoted in Oliver Strunk, *Source Readings,* 528. Marcello (b. 1686) was one of the most gifted composers of the Italian Baroque.

If a second singer objects to their status, Marcello recommends writing out ornamentation to the extent that her part has an equal number of notes as the prima donna.

The freedom of singers to augment the communication of emotions through improvisation over long notes of the melody, which corresponded with the key emotional words of the text, quickly led to excesses and later opera became a vehicle for the virtuoso singer. This too becomes a subject for Marcello's humor.

> If nouns such as "father," "empire," "love," "arena," "kingdom," "beauty," "courage," "heart," appear in the aria, the modern composer should write long coloraturas over them. This applies also to "no," "without," "already," and other adverbs. This serves to introduce a little change from the old custom of using coloratura passages only over words expressing motion or emotion, for instance "torment," "sorrow," "song," "fly," "fall."[42]

[42] Ibid., 49.

For the modern reader, perhaps the most surprising general information regarding improvisation are indications of an apparent indifference to form itself. Frescobaldi, in 1635, recommends that the organist "in the canzoni and ricercari may finish at any cadence, should the pieces seem too long."[43] In two other publications he makes similar comments.

> In the Toccatas I have attempted to offer not only a variety of passagework and expressive ornaments but also to make the various sections such that they can be played independently, so that the performer may stop wherever he wishes and not have to play the entire toccata...
>
> In the cadences, even though written in notes of small values, one must sustain them. As the performer approaches the end of a *passaggio* or cadence, the tempo must become more *adagio*.
>
> It is left to the good taste and fine judgment of the performer to decide the tempo that best suits the spirit and perfection of the manner and style of interpretation.[44]
>
> ......
>
> If the work should appear too fatiguing to play from beginning to end, one might begin a passage wherever he most pleases and end with a passage that finishes in the same mode.
>
> The beginning should be played slowly to give greater spirit and beauty to the following passages.[45]

Finally, Agostino Agazzari, in 1606, makes a few interesting comments of a more subjective nature about the strings:

> The lute in a concerto should be played with pleasing inventiveness and diversity, at times with firm strokes and with soft repercussions, at other times with broad passage work... and with groppi, trills, and accents to make it very attractive...
>
> The viols should be played with full bowing, clear and sonorous...
>
> The violin demands clear and lengthy runs, with scherzi, echoes, and responses, fughette, repetitions in different keys... with groppi and varied trills...
>
> Let it suffice for me to say to you that what is said here should be applied with prudence, warning the organists, the singers, and the ensemble to give each other room, not being offended by the multitude, but with ear and judgment waiting

[43] Frescobaldi, *Fiori musicali* (1635), quoted in Sam Morgenstern, *Composers on Music* (New York: Pantheon, 1956), 26. Frescobaldi (1583–1643) was one of the best known organists of Italy in the seventeenth century. Called to St. Peter's in Rome as organist in 1608, it was said his first performance drew 30,000 listeners.

[44] Frescobaldi, "Toccate e partite d'intavolatura," quoted in Carol MacClintock, *Readings in the History of Music in Performance*, 133ff.

[45] Frescobaldi, "Capricci fatti sopra diversi soggetti," quoted in Ibid., 135.

for the time and the place, and not act as though the passage at any one time belongs to the one who shouts the loudest.[46]

On Ornaments

We will not include here the extensive technical comments on the performance of specific ornaments found in Baroque treatises. We are interested, however, in comments which offer hints on the perception of the aesthetic use of these ornaments. The great Italian violin virtuoso, Geminiani, seemed particularly concerned with the aesthetic nature of ornaments. Of the appoggiatura, for example, he observes,

> The superior appoggiatura is supposed to express Love, Affection, Pleasure, etc. It should be made pretty long, giving it more than half the length or time of the note it belongs to … If it be made short, it will lose much of the aforesaid qualities.[47]

He discusses the mordent from the same perspective of the communication of feeling in performance.

> If it be performed with strength, and continued long, it expresses Fury, Anger, Resolution, etc. If it be played less strong and shorter, it expresses Mirth, Satisfaction, etc. But if you play it quite soft and swell the note, it may then denote Horror, Fear, Grief, Lamentation, etc. By making it short and swelling the note gently, it may express Affection and Pleasure.[48]

Geminiani also suggests the style of vibrato could convey either Majesty and Dignity or Affliction and Fear.[49]

It is interesting that Geminiani still considered the basic dynamic markings of *piano* and *forte* to be, like ornaments, subject to the will of the performer.

> They are both extremely necessary to express the intention of the melody; and as all good music should be composed in imitation of a discourse, these two ornaments are designed to produce the same effects that an orator does by raising and falling his voice.[50]

[46] Agostino Agazzari, Letter of 1606, quoted in Carol MacClintock, *Readings in the History of Music in Performance*, 131ff.

[47] Francesco Geminiani, *A Treatise of Good Taste in the Art of Musick* [1749] (New York: Da Capo Press, 1969), 2.

[48] Ibid., 3.

[49] Ibid.

[50] Ibid. See also under "Resources," the essay "The Maxime Principle" at www.maximesmusic.com.

Tosi also offers a few clues regarding the aesthetic quality of ornaments. The use of crescendo and diminuendo on a single pitch, which Tosi calls *Messa di Voce*, never fails to have "an exquisite effect" when used on an open vowel.[51] The *divisions*, contends Tosi,

[51] P. F. Tosi, *Observations*, I, xxix.

> do not have the power to touch the soul, but the most they can do is to raise our admiration of the singer for the happy flexibility of his voice.[52]

[52] Ibid., IV, i.

Divisions are only beautiful, he says, if they are in tune, accented, equal, distinct and fast. Like trills, if they are used too often they become "tedious, if not odious."[53]

[53] Ibid., IV, xixff.

A rarely discussed ornament mentioned by Tosi is the "drag." In this ornament, the singer begins on a high note and slowly "drags" the pitch down to a low note, making a diminuendo at the same time from *forte* to *piano* and stopping on some notes in the middle on the way down. "Every good musician takes it for granted," says Tosi, that no other ornament is "more apt to touch the heart."[54]

[54] Ibid., X, xxviii.

Tosi was particularly sensitive to ornaments and improvisation at cadences. He objected to trills:

> It grows abominable, when the singer persists with his tiresome warbling, nauseating the judicious, who suffer the more, because they know that the composers leave generally in every final cadence some note, sufficient to make a discreet embellishment . . . ,[55]

[55] Ibid., VIII, xiv.

and even a simple anticipation at a cadence, for "it hurts the ears and is against the rules."[56]

[56] Ibid., VIII, xii.

His greatest artistic objection was to the cadenza, which as the word reminds us was an extended cadence during the Baroque. For Tosi, extended solo improvisation at the cadence, especially in the da capo aria form, was inconsistent with high art.

> Every aria has (at least) three cadences that are final. Generally speaking, the study of the singers of the present times consist in terminating the cadence of the first part with an overflowing of passages and divisions at pleasure, and the orchestra waits; in that of the second the dose is increased, and

the orchestra grows tired; but on the last cadence, the throat is set a going like a weather-cock in a whirlwind, and the orchestra yawns. But why must the world be thus continually deafened with so many divisions?[57]

[57] Ibid., VIII, vff.

Answering his own question, Tosi suggests it is merely "begging for applause from the blind ignorant." But, he warns, singers in so doing damage the profession by such practices which are unworthy of the talent given them.

We will close this essay with a beautiful poem which is a virtual ode to performance. We quote a passage from Marino's *Adonis*, a musical contest. If this musical contest differs from the model of those of the ancient poets in the absence of the official judges, it surpasses all earlier examples in its poignant description and ultimate tragedy. Here we find an unhappy lover is singing in the forest, "in piteous sounds that gave vent unto his grief."[58] A nightingale hears him and begins to imitate his music, which leads to a contest in performance. Marino now gives us an unusually detailed picture of the passionate performance by the unhappy lover.

[58] Ibid., VII, 40ff.

> The skilled musician, viewing scornfully
> the competition of this challenger,
> and angry that a creature so minute
> not only matches but surpasses him,
> begins to search out on the lute the tones
> most difficult played on the highest frets;
> the eloquent, loquacious little tongue
> persistent follows, always copies him.
>
> The master reddens with disgust and shame
> to have been vanquished by a thing so mean.
> He turns the keys, sweeps up and down the strings,
> sounds chords in series mounting to the rose.
> Defiantly the warbler never stops,
> but renders each response more vigorously;
> and as the youth diminishes or soars,
> he deftly weaves the vocal labyrinth.

Astonished now, the lad became like ice
and irate said: "I've suffered thee awhile.
Now either thou wilt fail what I perform,
or I'll confess defeat and break my lute."
He grasped the hollow case tight in his arms,
and as to make a final proof of skill,
with tremolo and syncopy and fugue,
he sought all manner of variety.

Without a pause he strikes, releases, strikes
upon the neck from base to topmost fret,
and as his mood directs he murmurs low,
then swells the tone and plays in style sublime.
Sometimes he vibrates on the treble string,
while pressing with his thumb the major chord;
at other times with gravity profound
he plunges to the bordon's lowest depths.

His hand flies over the strings, now low, now high,
more nimble than the bird itself the hand;
first up, then down, with unexpected leaps
the speeding fingers move in lively dance.
Inimitably he imitates the stress
of fiery conflict and confused assault,
and equals with the sound of his sweet songs
the bellicose uproar and clash of arms.

Trumpets and timpani, such instruments
As Mars employs when marshaling the troops,
with whirlwind roar accelerating fierce,
his art expresses in skilled melody,
and all the while he plays he multiplies
the tempest of roulades in every part;
and while he thus compounds the harmonies,
his small competitor makes no response.

This musical duel continues for many hours until "the poor bird, exhausted finally, languished, fainted, weakened, and then died." The youth was much moved by the death of his competitor and, used his lute as a sepulcher to bury the bird,

Then with the feathers of the bird itself
he wrote the history of the event.

Finally, Marino includes some reflections on the ancient tradition of sung poetry, which makes one wonder to what degree in the seventeenth century poetry was still being sung. Particularly interesting here are the kinds of aesthetic purposes he gives, as well as the reference to the "music of the spheres."

> Music and Poesy are sisters twain,
> restorers of afflicted human kind,
> with power through happy rhymes to make serene
> the turbid tempests of our guilty thoughts.
> There are no arts more beautiful than these
> or more salubrious for troubled minds;
> wild Scythia holds no barbarous heart, except
> the tiger's, that sweet singing does not charm.
>
> . . . . . .
>
> Whoever harkens as the graceful hand
> strikes on the strings of the expressive lyre,
> wedding that music's charming melody
> with brilliant voices in a sweet accord,
> and does not sometimes feel the mighty power
> of those same numbers penetrate his heart,
> must have a spirit dissonant, that for
> the music of the spheres is out of tune.[59]

[59] Giambattista Marino, *L'Adone* [1623], trans. Harold Priest (Ithaca: Cornell University Press, 1967), VII, 1-2, 10. Marino (1569–1625) was a genuine court poet, working for a cardinal, a duke, a queen regent and a king of France.

4
Kircher on Music

THE MOST INTERESTING WRITER in seventeenth century Italy on the nature of music was Athanasius Kircher (1601–1680), a German born scholar who spent most of his adult life in Rome. Kircher began his theological studies in 1625 in Mainz and was ordained a priest in 1628. He obtained the chair of ethics and mathematics at the University of Würzburg, which included responsibility for giving instructions in the Syrian and Hebrew languages. However, the disorders of the Thirty Years War caused him to move to Lyons, in France, and later to Avignon.

The discovery of some hieroglyphic characters in the library at Speyer led Kircher to make his first attempt to solve the problem of hieroglyphical writing, which still baffled all scholars. An important collector with influence in Rome arranged for Kircher to go to Rome to work in this field. On his way, however, he was shipwrecked near Cività Vecchia. Eventually he arrived in Rome, where he would remain for the rest of his life.

After six years of successful teaching in the Roman College, where he lectured on physics, mathematics, and Oriental languages, he was released from these duties that he might have freedom in his studies and might devote himself to formal scientific research, especially in Southern Italy and Sicily. He took advantage of a trip to Malta to explore thoroughly the various volcanoes which exist between Naples and that island. He studied especially in 1638 the Strait of Messina, where, besides the noise of the surf, a dull subterranean rumble attracted his attention to such mysterious phenomena as the frightful eruption of Vesuvius in 1630.

When Kircher left Messina in 1638 to return to Naples, a terrible earthquake occurred which destroyed the city of Euphemia. Like Pliny before him (AD 79), Kircher wished to study at close range this powerful convulsion of nature. On reaching Naples he at once climbed Vesuvius, and had himself lowered by means of a rope into the crater of the volcanic mountain and with the help of his pantometer ascertained exactly the different dimensions of the crater and its inner structure.

His great work on music was the *Musurgia Universalis* (Rome, 1650), a virtual encyclopedia of music. While he appears to have been widely read himself, he also cites a number of scholars in Rome with whom he consulted in the preparation of his work. He also acknowledged, in his preface, his indebtedness to Mersenne's *Harmonie Universelle*, although he says the latter was more addressed to the philosopher than the practical musician.

Some critics had apparently questioned his authority to write on the subject of music, as Kircher admits in his preface.

> I hear, among other things, that this objection is made to me: "How can the author have the audacity, since he is not a musician by profession, to undertake to correct and emend masters in the art, brought up in it almost from the cradle, and what is uppermost, to place himself as master over them, with more audacity than modesty?" To these I answer that I am certainly not and have never been a musician by profession, since it is a calling not appropriate to my religion.[1]

Kircher continues, somewhat sarcastically, saying that what his critics mean, when they say he is not a professional musician, is that he has not taught music to boys in school, conducted a church choir or been a mercenary by writing for money. On the other hand, he notes,

[1] Athanasius Kircher, *Musurgia universalis* [1650], trans. Frederick Crane (unpublished dissertation, State University of Iowa, 1956), xix.

> From an early age I have devoted my attention not only to more distinguished arts and sciences, but also to the practice of music, with the most thorough study and steadfast labor; and let [the critics] have no doubt that I have not been concerned with musical speculation only, since various compositions printed in Germany, but under the name of others, are passed around to the greatest pleasure of listeners and held in esteem.

Kircher's *Musurgia Universalis* is divided into ten books, the first of which he entitles, "Anatomical." The earliest Greek philosophers, indeed philosophy as we know it, began with attempts to explain the physical world. They soon fixed four basic elements (air, water, fire and earth) and four qualities (hot, cold, moist and dry). Attempts to relate man to the physical world resulted in the theory of the four "humors," sanguine, phlegmatic, choleric and melancholic, the balance of which determined a person's disposition, character and life style. Athanasius Kircher believed the humors indigenous to a person explained his preferences in music.

> Melancholy people like grave, solid, and sad harmony; sanguine person prefer the *hyporchematic* style (dance music) because it agitates the blood; choleric people like agitated harmonies because of the vehemence of their swollen gall; martially inclined men are partial to trumpets and drums and reject all delicate and pure music; phlegmatic persons lean toward women's voices because their high pitched voice has a benevolent effect on phlegmatic humour.[2]

Since it had long been assumed that these humors, and thus the person, could be affected by external influences, many philosophers also assumed that it was here that the power of music on the listener was found. Some seventeenth century philosophers attempted to explain the influence of music on the affections, but, because language can explain neither music nor the emotions, their writings were largely unheeded by practical musicians.

Kircher began by determining that there are eight basic emotions which music can affect: love, grief or pain, joy,

[2] Athanasius Kircher, *Musurgia Universalis*, quoted in Paul Henry Lang, "Musical Thought of the Baroque: The Doctrine of Temperaments and Affections," in *Twentieth-Century Views of Music History*, ed. William Hays (New York: Scribner's, 1972), 195.

exultancy, rage or indignation, compassion or tears, fear or distress, presumption or audacity and admiration or astonishment.[3] The philosophers in Germany tried to equate such emotions with specific elements of music, which was an effort doomed to failure since individual elements, such as intervals, for example, express little in comparison with how they are used by the composer. Very much to the dismay of those who demand more scientific sounding concepts, Kircher attempted to identify the power of music at work through descriptive, and even subjective, language. For the first emotion, love [*paradigma affectus amoris*] he finds in a madrigal by Gesualdo intervals which languish and syncopations which express "the syncope of the languishing heart." The second emotion, grief or pain [*paradigma affectus dolorosi*] he illustrates by describing the lament of Jephtha's daughter in an oratorio by Carissimi.

[3] *Musurgia Universalis*, I, Bk. I, iii, 6.

> Giacomo Carissimi, a very excellent and famous composer ... through his genius and the felicity of his compositions, surpasses all others in moving the minds of listeners to whatever affection he wishes. His compositions are truly imbued with the essence and life of the spirit. Among numerous works of great worth, he has composed the dialogue of Jephte ... After the recitative with which he ingeniously and subtly expresses the jubilant welcome accorded Jephtha by his daughter (who celebrates the victories and triumphs of her father in a joyous dance, accompanied by all sorts of musical instruments), Carissimi depicts, by means of a sudden change of mode, the dismay into which Jephtha has been plunged by this unexpected meeting with his only begotten daughter, against whom he has taken an irrevocable vow, and whom he despairs of being able to save. Joy thus gives way to the opposing affections of sorrow and grief. This is followed by the six-voice lament of the daughter's virgin companions, which Carissimi composes with such skill that you would swear you could hear their sobbings and lamentations. Having, in fact, begun with a festive dialogue, cast in the dance-like tone 8, Carissimi sets this lament in a very different mode, in this case tone 4 intermingled with tone 3. Given this tragic story to portray—a story in which joy is dispelled by the distress and intense sorrow of the heart—the composer suitably chose a mode that is as distant from tone 8 as are the extremes of the

heavens from each other, that he might better express, through this opposition, the differences between the affections. And nothing is more capable than this of portraying such unhappy events, such tragic happenings interwoven with affections of a different kind.

Here he also deals with the nature of the production of vocal sounds, including those by animals, birds and insects, presenting in many cases their calls in musical notation. Of all the animals he discusses, he was most fascinated by the [Central] American sloth,[4] which Kircher understood sang, to the syllable "ha," the diatonic scale.

> It perfectly intones as learners do, the first elements of music, *do, re, me, fa, sol, la, sol, fa, me, re, do*. Ascending and descending through the common intervals of the six degrees, insomuch that the Spaniards, when they first took possession of these coasts, and perceived such a kind of vociferation in the night, thought they heard men accustomed to the rules of music.

Kircher concluded,

> If music were first invented in America, I would say that it must have begun with the amazing voice of this animal.

Book Two, "Philological," consists of studies of music in the ancient civilizations, in particular Hebrew and Greek.

Book Three, "Arithmetical," concerns traditional music theory as it was developed by Church philosophers during the Middle Ages. Here he also presents a system of "musical arithmetic," through which the rules of addition, subtraction, multiplication and division of intervals are represented by special characters.

Book Four, "Geometrical," deals with the monochord, with geometric and algebraic systems for determining the intervals.

Book Five, "Symphonurgic," consists of rules for composing music in the old church style [*stile antico*].

Book Six, "Organic music," the medieval term for instrumental music, discusses as well geometry and acoustics. Here Kircher deals with the physical characteristics of the

[4] Kircher gives a description of this animal which he says is named from the fact that in fifteen days it does not travel as far as one can throw a spear.

No one knows what meat it feeds on... they for the most part keep on the tops of trees... [With their feet] they have such strength, that whatsoever animal they lay hold on they keep it so fast, that it is never after able to free itself from their nails, but it is compelled to die through hunger. On the other hand, this beast so greatly affects the men that are coming towards it by its countenance, that in pure compassion they refrain from molesting it, and easily persuade themselves not to be solicitous about that which nature has subjected to so defenseless and miserable a state of body.

family of instruments, but, unfortunately, includes little information on performance practice or of aesthetic considerations. He makes the inaccurate assumption that string instruments must be the most ancient,[5] partly because of their prominence in the Old Testament, but also because he assumes man always had available cords (potential musical strings) to tie things with.[6]

It is somewhat unexpected that Kircher tells us that the cornett was missing in mid seventeenth century Rome, since it was a common instrument at the end of the sixteenth century.

> Since the cornetts attain a remarkable power in music, I certainly wonder that our Roman musicians take no interest in them, since nothing could be more suited to church music, especially if three, four, or five cornetts are accompanied by a bassoon. I certainly would think that ensembles of this sort, from time to time, would be much preferred to string ensembles for major solemnities and festivities.[7]

We like a comment by Kircher made as part of his explanation of the distribution of the natural tones of the trumpet:

> You see, therefore, how much nature abhors dissonances, so that the trumpet would rather burst than allow them.[8]

He also makes a brief reference to improvisation in the highest trumpet part, a subject relatively little discussed during the seventeenth century. This is due in part to the rather secretive nature of the trumpet guilds and their repertoire of memorized, and rarely notated, music.

> There remains an explanation of the style of music that trumpets perform ... Since all instruments require different styles of compositions, it will certainly be most obvious of an ensemble of trumpets. And it is established for four trumpets that the first of them carries the top part, indulging in various *clausulae* and diminutions. Two others take the middle road; the fourth, which they also call the *bourdon*, remaining on a continuous unison, serves, as it were, in place of a bass. There are those, moreover, who use the trumpets that are called *clarinas* just the same as flutes for any kind of ensemble, and perform the soprano parts perfectly with all the diminutions displayed.[9]

---

[5] Logic would suggest instruments made of natural objects, such as flutes from bones, percussion instruments from turtle shells and trumpets from sea shells, must be older than string instruments which require a relatively advanced technology to make.

[6] Kircher, *Musurgia universalis,* trans. Crane, 1.

[7] Ibid., 91.

[8] Ibid., 94.

[9] Ibid., 96ff.

Kircher mentions the peasant bagpipe which, he says, is "the only solace of shepherds and peasants." The new bagpipe designed for use by the court in Paris, the musette, he finds is "marvelous to hear."

> Here at Rome I have seen an instrument of this sort not without a singular delight to my soul.[10]

[10] Ibid., 99ff.

He includes in the discussion of the bagpipe the other double reeds, hautbois and dulcian.

> But among them the one that is called *fagot* in the vernacular especially stands out; nothing sweeter or more fitted for playing the bass can be imagined.[11]

[11] Ibid., 100.

Following the wind instruments, Kircher discusses the organ and he is one of few writers who acknowledge the organ for what it really was in the Baroque: a surrogate wind band.

> The organ is like a sort of epitome and compendium of all wind instruments, and thus is deservedly the most beautiful and perfect of all.[12]

[12] Ibid., 102.

In discussing the skins used for percussion instruments, Kircher relates a charming contemporary example of folklore about sheep.

> Just one little sheep feeds us, clothes us, and entertains us with four types of musical instruments, with intestines for strings, with shinbones and horns for pipes, and finally the skin turning into a drum, so that consequently the Hebrews have declared of it not inelegantly that the live animal has one voice; dead, seven.[13]

[13] Ibid., 161.

Finally, after discussing an instrument much like the modern xylophone, Kircher is reminded of a most curious anecdote—or should we say, tale!

> Not so long ago, in order to dispel the melancholy of some great prince, a noted and ingenious actor constructed an instrument such as this. He took live cats all of different sizes, and shut them up in a kind of box especially made for this business, so that their tails, stuck through the holes, were

inserted tightly into certain channels. Under these he put keys fitted with the sharpest points instead of mallets. Then he arranged the cats tonally according to their different sizes, so that each key corresponded to the tail of one cat, and he put the instrument prepared for the relaxation of the prince in a suitable place. Then when it was played, it produced such music as the voices of cats can produce. For when the keys, depressed by the fingers of the organist, pricked the tails of the cats with their points, they, driven to a rage, with miserable voices, howling now low, now high, produced such music made of the voices of cats as would move men to laughter and even arouse shrews to dance.[14]

[14] Ibid., 138ff.

Book Seven, "Diacritical," contains additional material on the ancient civilizations, the development of music during the Middle Ages and discussions of the classification of styles. Following the publication in 1643 of Marco Scacchi's *Cribrum musicum ad triticum Syferticum*, several critics adopted his classification of music in three functional divisions: church, chamber and theater. Kircher presented a much more extensive classification of music, discussing first what he called "individual styles" of music, ideas which based on the so-called "humors." His second classification had to do with "national styles." The third classification followed Scacchi's concept of a function-based system, but Kircher's is more extended, with eight categories.

Stylus ecclesiasticus, church style with or without chant. This must be "full of majesty, miraculously transporting the heart to contemplation of the solemn and grave, imprinting on the heart its own motion." *Stylus motecticus* is a sub-category, with more varied and florid style.

Stylus canonicus [canon], in which the "musical ability of a composer is shown at its most skillful."

Stylus phantasticus [improvisation], which Kircher finds "an extremely free and uninhibited method of composition particularly suitable for instrumental music." He cites here the toccata, ricercar, fantasias and sonatas.

Stylus madrigalecus, "Italian style par excellence, joyful, lively, full of sweetness and grace, lending itself easily to vocal diminutions, and eschewing slowness of movement, unless specifically required by the text." This style, he says, is suitable for the portrayal of love, affection and pain.

Stylus melismaticus, "particularly appropriate for measured verses and meters ... sweetly sung without agitation or affected dissonance."

Stylus hyporchematicus, for feasts and festivities and *Stylus choraicus,* for dance and ballet. This style has the ability to "excite emotions of joy, exaltation, wantonness and licentiousness."

Stylus symphoniacus, instrumental music.

Stylus dramaticus or *Stylus recitativus,* recitative style for the representation of any of the so-called affections, or for abrupt changes of affection through sudden alternations in tonality, the so-called *Stylus metabolicus.*[15]

[15] Quoted in Ibid., 50.

Book Eight, "Miraculous Musicology," concerns time, including the poetic meters in a number of languages and a system by which the "unskilled in music can attain a perfect knowledge of composing in a short time." Kircher includes in this book reproductions of a song composed by Louis XIII of France and a five-part madrigal by the emperor Ferdinand III.

Book Nine, "The Magic of Consonance and Dissonance," in which "the secrets of all the science of music are brought into the light by countless experiments." Certainly one of the most interesting parts of his work, we find here many curious and interesting things.

First, he is credited with being the person who originated the idea of playing music on drinking glasses, which was the result of his experimentation in observing the effects of the tones produced by glasses filled with wine, water, seawater and oil, etc. This led him to acoustics in general, in the course of which he concluded that the biblical account of the fall of the walls of Jericho was not due to the sound of the trumpets, but some other physical cause.

In this book Kircher also discusses the effects of music on the mind and the use of music therapy. Here he discusses the use of music to cure the bite of the Tarantula spider, something widely mentioned in early literature.[16] Kircher cites several histories of this phenomenon, including a girl who was bitten and was cured by the music of only a drum. In another case, however, he reports a volunteer allowed himself to be bitten by two Tarantulas, of different colors. As the bite of one responded to music and dance, but the bite of the other was made worse, the patient died. Kircher's technical explanation reads,

> The poison is sharp, gnawing, and bilious and is received and incorporated into the medullary substances of the fibers. The music has the power to rarefy the air to a certain harmonic pitch; the air thus rarefied, penetrating the pores of the patient's body, affects the muscles, arteries, and minute fibers, and incites him to dance, which begets a perspiration, in which the poison evaporates.

Kircher also devotes considerable space in Book Nine to echoes, beginning with a lovely anecdote.

> A certain friend of mine having set out on a journey, had a river to cross, and not knowing the stream, cried out *Oh*, to which an echo answered *Oh;* he imagining it to be a man, called out in Italian, *Onde devo passar?* it answered *passa;* and when he asked *qui?* it replied *qui;* but as the waters formed a deep whirlpool there, and made a great noise, he was terrified, and again asked *Devo passar qui?* The echo returns *passa qui.* He repeated the same question often, and still had the same answer. Terrified with the fear of being obliged to swim in case he attempted to pass there, and it being a dark and tempestuous night, he concluded that his respondent was some evil spirit that wanted to entice him into the torrent.

In the course of this discussion, Kircher cites a building in Pavia which would return an echo thirty times.

In this book Kircher also mentions a number of curious mechanical musical instruments, including a Cymbalarian, a machine consisting of revolving bells, and a combination of a hurdy-gurdy and a harpsichord which produced the impression of a consort of viols. One device of his own invention was a wooden box, strung with gut strings, which,

---

[16] In another book, *Magnes siue De arte magnetica opus tripartitum* (Rome, 1641) Kircher also discusses "the magnetic power and faculties of music" and "the affections of the mind which music excites." Here again, of particular interest is a special science which he calls "Tarantism," the study of the "magnetism and amazing sympathy with music" of the tarantula.

when placed in a window, produced sounds generated by the wind.

> The method of tuning it, which is not, as in other instruments, by thirds, fourths, fifths, or eighths, but all the chords are to be tuned by an unison, or in octaves. It is very wonderful, and nearly paradoxical, that chords thus tuned should constitute different harmony. This musical phenomenon has not as yet been observed by any one that I know of ...
>
> When it is thus disposed you will perceive an harmony in the room in proportion as the wind is weaker or stronger; for from time to time all the chords having a tremulous motion impressed upon them, produce a correspondent variety of sounds, resembling a consort of pipes or flutes, affecting the hearers with a strange pleasure.

Just before his death, Kicher published a book called *Phonurgia Nova* (Rome, 1673) in which he describes his invention of a Speaking Trumpet, an idea which he says he took from the new telescopes. Among other demonstrations, he adapted it to a statue in an art gallery, shocking the viewers with "feigned and ludicrous consultations." He also claims he constructed one version on a mountain, where the sound traveled four miles and was taken by villagers as a voice from heaven telling them to climb the mountain to celebrate the feast of Pentecost.

Book Ten, "Decachord of Nature," focuses on the organ; the music of the spheres; the harmony of minerals, plants and animals with the heavens; political music; musical metaphysics; the music of angels and the harmony of nature.

5
On Court Music of the Italian Baroque

AT A TIME WHEN NUMEROUS ITALIAN MUSICIANS were being offered positions in courts abroad, those musicians who remained in Italy found themselves domestic servants to an aristocracy (including the nobles of the Church) which preferred to be entertained to being moved. Even Monteverdi, a genius who clearly saw the future of music and one of the very great musicians of the Baroque, spent much of his life working for nobles incapable of appreciating his ability. In one letter he complains that due to the pressure of composing music for a court wedding,

> I have had a frightful pain in my head and so terrible and violent an itching around my waist, that neither by cauteries which I have had applied to myself, nor by purges taken orally, nor by blood-letting and other potent remedies has it so far been possible to get even partly better. My father attributes the cause of the headache to mental strain.

Further, he complains that after suffering from cold, lack of clothing, servitude, and very nearly lack of food, at the wedding His Highness failed to compliment his work before the noble guests. Nevertheless, he concludes the letter, "I bow and kiss your hands."[1]

Pressed to compose music for a court allegorical pageant, he wearily wrote a Mantuan court official, "How can I, by such means, move the passions?"[2] In such an environment, the composer takes his joy where he can find it. Monteverdi

[1] Letter to Annibale Chieppio (December 2, 1608), quoted in *The Letters of Claudio Monteverdi,* trans. Denis Stevens (Cambridge: Cambridge University Press, 1980), 57ff.

[2] Ibid., 115ff.

wrote the music for an allegorical tournament celebrating the marriage of Duke Odoardo Farnese of Parma and Margherita de' Medici of Florence in 1628 and even he must have been pleased with a moment described by one eyewitness.

> As soon as Signora Settimia, representing Aurora, began to sing, all conversation among the spectators ceased ... All ears were so consoled by the sweetness of the voice and the divine quality of the song, that among the 10,000 people seated in the theater, there was no one ... who did not grow tender at the trills, sigh at the sighs, become ecstatic at the ornaments, and who was not stupefied and transfixed by the miraculous beauty and song of an heavenly siren.[3]

During the first part of the seventeenth century many court entertainments were of the allegorical type we associate with the sixteenth century, which only reminds us that, except for opera, most musical traditions passed into the seventeenth century, the people living then unmindful that the Baroque Period had arrived. Such an entertainment, a large-scale allegorical ballet, was given by the "Most Serene Infantas of Savoy, in honor of Madame of France," at the court in Turin in 1620.[4] An eyewitness reports that the evening began with a lavish banquet with music.

> These gastronomic pleasures were further enhanced by the sweetness of the music, which gave nourishment to the ears and filled the souls of those present with contentment.

This banquet concluded at midnight! Following a trumpet fanfare,

> The entire cloth was seen to disappear in a flash behind the clouds, revealing all at once such a quantity of wonderful and admirable things that many of those present were lost in amazement. In the first place, the scene depicted a parched Alpine mountain, with crags vegetated by nothing but a few nettles and briars among the cracks and stiff, unyielding and discolored grass. At the top of this mountain, the Temple of Glory shone out with brightest rays; this was made in crystal with columns of gold. In the middle, the Most Serene Infantas Maria and Caterina could be seen with twelve of their ladies dressed as queens. At the foot, in the middle, Toil

[3] Quoted in Tim Carter, "The North Italian Courts," in *The Early Baroque Era* (Englewood Cliffs: Prentice Hall, 1994), 39.

[4] This description is found in Lorenzo Bianconi, *Music in the Seventeenth Century*, trans. David Bryant (Cambridge: Cambridge University Press, 1987), 271ff.

wielded his bludgeon, striking down lions, serpents, wild
boars and sundry other beasts; at the base of the mountain,
Love, Indolence, Oblivion, Sloth, Slumber, Gluttony, Sin and
Pleasure sleepily and lazily kept watch.

Now, the allegorical character, "Toil," sang a madrigal.

> He who treads the flowery path
> Of tyrant pleasure
> Finally will wretched fall,
> Deceived, in the bottomless pit of everlasting loss ...

Following this song, the allegorical ensemble, "the Sins"
began a ballet.

> The cornetts and trombones took up a broken melody with
> artfully contrived retardations, to which rhythm the Sins
> recommenced their ballet ... in perfect measure and in such
> perfect time as to leave an indelible impression on the minds
> of those present.

Now "Heroic Virtue" sang a song, followed with another
song by Apollo. Next the Muses "added their full chorus of
voices" prior to an appearance of "the Poets" and another
ballet.

> To the sound of a grave and dramatic harmony they formed a
> most graceful ballet with unsurpassable elegance and design.

Following the ballet and a song by the character, "Glory,"
the temple of Glory was slowly exposed from inside the
mountain. Suddenly an arch rose, upon which were seated
Victory, Fame and Honor. Now, holding her scepter, Glory
sang again,

> Go forth, ye who earned,
> On the path of toil,
> The laurels of Glory ...

After an hour, the ballet concluded with "a most beautiful
ballet of forty figures," to the music of violins, followed by
all the singers and instrumentalists joining together for "a
melody of extraordinary sweetness." The ballet was over,

but not the dancing. The violins remained to play branles "and other favorite dances for the pleasure of the ladies and gentlemen present."

Among the entertainments popular with the aristocracy in seventeenth century Italy were the horse ballets, which also spread to Germany as "Ross Ballet" and to France as "Carrousel." These entertainments evolved as a replacement for the earlier tournaments, which had become too dangerous after the invention of firearms. Typically these horse ballets were given in the central plaza of the city, with great tiers of benches forming a stadium of sorts. There was usually a central allegorical theme (such as the early "War of Love" in 1615 in Florence), large constructed floats and military troops arranged in symmetrical formations. For one of these events in 1628, Monteverdi had to set 1,000 lines of text to music. He confesses in a letter than when he could no longer find "emotional variety, I tried to change the instrumentation."[5] The music most often consisted of the aristocratic trumpet and timpani corps, but since their repertoire was memorized, little has survived.

There was also a curious military relationship with these horse ballets, for in the previous centuries the problem of the organization and movement of large movements of troops had evolved into theories of complicated geometric patterns as the basis of attack and defense. Consequently Baroque military treatises often chart their formations on the basis of choreographic principles rather than from purely strategic logic. An example is Müller's *Trilekünst zu Fuss* (Lübeck, 1672) which recommends for the defense of Lübeck the placing of the troops in a configuration resembling the coat-of-arms of the city![6]

In Venice, instead of the horse ballet the public saw great water pageants sponsored by the aristocracy. In 1685, for example, a great naval "battle" was given in honor of the visiting Duke of Brunswick. This "battle" was fought between Venetian and Turkish galleys, with the former achieving a glorious victory. The musicians are described as 24 trumpets, oboes, drums and 36 singers.[7] The visiting Englishman, John

[5] Letter to Alessandro Striggio (February 4, 1628), quoted in *The Letters of Claudio Monteverdi*, 390.

[6] Paul Nettl, "Equestrian Ballets of the Baroque Period," *The Musical Quarterly* 19, no. 1 (Jan., 1933): 74. One can see examples of these figures in Machiavelli's *The Art of War*.

[7] Pompeo Molmenti, *Venice* (London, 1908), I, iii, 198.

Evelyn, observed the annual water procession on Ascension Day in 1645 and recalls,

> First the Doge, or Duke in his robes of State (which were very particular & after the Eastern) together with the Senate in their gownes, Imbarked in their gloriously painted, carved & gilded Bucentoro, [surrounded] & follow'd by innumerable Gallys, Gundolas, & boates filled with Spectators, some dressed in Masqurade, Trumpets, musique & Canons, filling the whole aire with din.[8]

[8] *The Diary of John Evelyn* (Oxford, 1955), II, 432.

Another great celebration on the water, this time on a river, was given for the wedding of Prince Cosimo, of the Medici, with the Hapsburg Archduchess Maria Magdalena. This spectacle, entitled, "The Argonauts on the Arno," included vast numbers of boats decorated as floats, a huge cast representing all the Greek gods, two fire-breathing bulls and a hissing dragon. The music included a group of nymphs and shepherds performing on wind instruments.[9]

[9] A. M. Nagler, *Theatre Festivals of the Medici* (New Haven, 1964), 115.

Monteverdi in a letter of 1627 mentions such a procession to celebrate a naval victory during which "solemn music" was sung.[10]

[10] Letter to Enzo Bentivoglio (September 25, 1627), quoted in *The Letters of Claudio Monteverdi*, 370.

Continuing the Renaissance custom, many nobles continued to maintain high quality musical establishments. An extant letter of Monteverdi reveals that he had been instructed by the court at Mantua to lure away a five-member wind band currently employed by the Spanish governor of Milan. Monteverdi describes their abilities, indicating they do equally well in functional and concert music, and makes recommendations regarding their salary.[11] We get a glimpse of the range of duties for such a wind band in a letter several years later, when Monteverdi is again commissioned to find a player. Monteverdi, in reporting on his conversation with a prospective player, says he told him,

[11] Letter to Alessandro Striggio (August 24, 1609), Ibid., 64.

> If His Highness the Prince were pleased to take you on, this gentleman very much likes not only to hear a variety of wind instruments, he also likes to have the said musicians play in private, in church, in procession, and atop city walls; now madrigals, now French songs, now airs, and now dance songs.[12]

[12] Letter to Prince Francesco Gonzaga (March 26, 1611), Ibid., 81.

In a letter of 1623 he reports that while good wind players are in abundance, he cannot find suitable soprani or continuo players and only a moderate theorbo player.[13] In numerous other letters Monteverdi reports back on prospective singers, discussing in detail their artistic and vocal qualities.

The Italian nobles also had their private trumpet players and a few of their names are known today, in particular Girolamo Fantini, who served under the Grand Duke Ferdinando II of Florence. Fantini's famous trumpet treatise was no doubt taken from his eight years' experience in this court. Another famous trumpeter in this same court was the German known as Simone di Lionardo.[14]

One may be sure these aristocratic trumpeters appeared in all major court festivities. The marriage of Ereditario in Florence, in 1661, included a ceremonial coronation of the new bride by Ferdinando II, a horse ballet and firing of artillery. Perhaps one sees the duke's personal trumpets in a document which mentions twelve trombetti, dressed in crimson velvet preceding the sergeant general and the "other" trumpets.[15] A similar scene occurred when Vittorio Amedeo II of Torino returned with his new bride, Anna d'Orleans, niece to Louis XIV, from their wedding in France. They were welcomed from the Beauvoisin bridge by a great number of trumpets and timpani.[16]

Among the most comprehensive of the records of music in the courts of nobles during the Italian Baroque are the records of the ensembles of the popes. They, too, had their aristocratic trumpets, called *concerto de' 4 trombetti dell'Inclito Popolo Romano,* in 1717. There were four principal members with two alternates called *coadiutori* and *sopranumerari.* A position for a timpanist, as part of this ensemble, was made official in 1734, but one was undoubtedly used before that date. The Statutes of 1717 state that their first obligation was to the pope and provided additional funds for the persons who cared for their horses, their clothes and their barbers. They had a specific rate of six *giulii* per day if they were hired to appear in university or diplomatic ceremonies. Otherwise, if they agreed to perform for private individuals, they had

[13] Ibid., 266.

[14] Alessandro Vessella, *La Banda* (Milan, 1935), 94.

[15] Gaetano Imbert, *La vita fiorentina nel '600* (Firenze, 1906), 75ff.

[16] Luisa Saredo, "Il Matrimonio di Vittorio Emanuele II su documenti inediti," in *Nuova Antologia* (1885), XLI, fasc. ix.

to be content with the money offered by the sponsor; if they complained, in this regard, they were subject to a fine. The Statutes of 1734 deal with the additional problems of discipline, abusiveness and fighting among themselves.[17]

[17] Vessella, *La Banda*, 115ff.

There was a separate papal ensemble called *Tamburini del Popolo Romano*, which consisted of eight principal players and a number of official alternates. The oldest member was the leader, *Capo tamburo*, who carried the flag of the pope and was responsible for the quality of the performance. He also arranged for alternate players in case of illness. These percussionists performed for all public ceremonies involving the pope, cardinals, ambassadors and the mayor. They were paid six *giulii* per day and were provided with official uniforms. One document of 1758 warns the ensemble that their new uniform must last six years.[18]

[18] Ibid., 116–120, with sources for numerous contemporary documents.

Following the tradition of the great dukes of Italy, the pope also maintained a personal wind band, housed in the *Castel Sant' Angelo*. In papal documents they are called the *musici del concerto di Campidoglio* in 1702 and the *Concerto de tromboni e cornetti del Senato et inclito Popolo Romano* and sometimes just *Concerto Capitolino* in 1705. Their constitution requires a leader, the *Priore*, who was to be elected month by month by the players and who was responsible for their repertoire, performance and pay. Members were cautioned against blasphemy and urged to show the necessary respect for their colleagues. An ensemble of eight players, six trombones and two cornetts, they performed for the usual public ceremonies and also for the meals of the *Sig. Conservatori*.[19]

[19] Ibid., 103–4, 110–111.

Surviving documents relative to the coronations of popes mentions the use of trumpets on horse and timpani for Urbano VIII (1623); six *tubicines* and timpani as well as the papal *trombetti* for Innocenzo X in 1644; ten *tamburini* in rich velvet crimson cassocks trimmed in gold and the four *trombetti del Popolo Romano* in red, trimmed in gold for Clemente IX in 1667; *timpano del Popolo Romano* for Clemente X in 1670; *tamburini* in rich cassocks and the *trombetti del Popolo Romano* in red, for Innocenzo XI in 1676; ten *tamburini* and four trumpets for Alessandro VIII in 1689, Innocenzo XII in 1691 and Clemente XI in 1700.[20]

In addition the popes, dukes and lesser nobles were active in sponsoring concerts during seventeenth century Italy. Sometimes these consisted of opera, given in private palace theaters, or as in Venice, concerts sponsored by aristocratic "academies." In Rome the cardinals and other Church princes were especially involved in the support of music, sometimes taking a personal role. Benedetto Pamphili (1653–1730), grand nephew to pope Innocent X, wrote the libretto for *Il trionfo del Tempo e del Disinganno*, the first oratorio of Handel. In a letter of 1620, Monteverdi mentions his *Lament of Apollo* being performed during a regular series of one-hour concerts held in the home of a "certain gentleman of the Bembo family, where the most important ladies and gentlemen come to listen."[21]

In speaking of the aristocratic patronage of music in Italy, one cannot pass by Christina of Sweden (1626–1689) who arrived in Rome in 1656 and became the center of intellectual and musical life there for the next thirty-three years. In Christina we have one of the most remarkable women in history. She might well carry off the prize for best mind, among all past European rulers, male or female.

Her father was the highly educated, courteous, generous and handsome Gustavus Adolphus of Sweden. He loved Christina dearly, but the mother, Maria Eleanora of Brandenburg, could not hide her disappointment that the child was a girl, and not a boy, heir. It seems clear that Christina was therefore driven to be both. She played the masculine role in dress, language, riding and hunting. A Spanish envoy reported, "She cannot bear the idea of marriage, because she was born free and will die free." It is more likely that she probably also knew she would be unable to find a husband her equal, indeed one wonders who, save another Leonardo da Vinci, he might have been.

Christina became queen at age eighteen in a burst of energy and display of self-discipline that must have caused

[20] Ibid., 125.

[21] Letter to Alessandro Striggio (February 1, 1620), quoted in *The Letters of Claudio Monteverdi*, 167.

astonishment in all who knew her. The above-mentioned envoy reported,

> She spends only three or four hours in sleep. When she wakes she spends five hours in reading ... She never drinks anything but water; never has she been heard to speak of her food, whether it was well or ill cooked ... Ambassadors speak only with her, without ever being passed on to a secretary or minister.

It is difficult to guess what she was reading those five hours, so extraordinary was the diversity of her interests. By age eighteen she spoke German, French, Italian, Spanish and Latin, later adding Greek, Hebrew and Arabic. She loved poetry and assembled a great library, which included rare manuscripts she collected. She brought, or attracted, scholars and thinkers of every field of science, philosophy and theology. She founded seven colleges and urged Swedish scholars to write in Swedish, in order that all her people might benefit. Who could disagree with Pascal, who said she was queen of the realm of mind, as well as of government, or with Milton who thought she should govern the entire world.

This great education brought her inevitably to philosophy, and so she brought to Stockholm the greatest philosopher of her age, René Descartes. Poor Descartes, who like all good philosophers preferred to sleep late, thought he might not survive her demand that their conversations began the day at 5:00 AM. In fact, making these early morning walks in the snow, he caught pneumonia and died. How rare it might have been to listen in on these conversations, listening as Christina questioned Descartes on Plato! Once when he contended that all animals are but mechanisms, she responded that she had never seen her watch give birth to baby watches! She left a manuscript containing her personal maxims, and we would like to think the first of these was in answer to Descartes' famous one, "I think, therefore I am."

> One is, in proportion as one can love.
> To undeceive men is to offend them.
> Extraordinary merit is a crime never forgiven.
> More courage is required for marriage than for war.

Philosophy neither changes men nor corrects men.

She began to become interested in Catholicism and in 1652 requested that several Jesuits come, in disguise, to discuss Catholic theology with her. In Sweden it was at this time impossible for her to become a Catholic and retain her crown, for her father had died to protect Protestantism. After much soul searching and negotiation she abdicated in 1654. She left Stockholm that night, dressed as a man, to begin a long trip to Italy.

In her passage through Italy she was welcomed in town after town like some modern victorious Caesar. She entered Rome riding on a white horse, through the triumphal arch and the Porta del Popolo, passing great crowds of soldiers and the public, to be welcomed by Alexander VII in the Vatican.

Christina began her new life with the joy of visiting museums, libraries and academies, astonishing all with her knowledge of Italian history and being entertained by the great families of Rome. Here also she founded the leading salon of Rome, bringing together prelates, scholars and composers. Among the latter she received Corelli, who dedicated his first publication of sonatas to her, and Scarlatti, whose operas she produced in her private theater. She collected art and books, which later became treasures of the Vatican Library, and led a movement to inspire Italian writers to return to the purity of language and expression found under the Medici.

Christina lived in one of the great palaces of Rome and remained at heart a queen. When she died in 1689, at age sixty-three, and was buried in St. Peter's, an Italian poet, Filicia, reflected that her kingdom consisted of "all those who thought, all those who acted, and all those who were endowed with intelligence."

Another foreign queen in Rome was Maria Casimira (1641–1716), widow of Jan III of Poland. Like Christina she established her local reputation by her support of the arts and as Christina had hired Alessandro Scarlatti as her *maestro di cappella*, Maria hired his son, Domenico Scarlatti.

The salons hosted by these aristocratic ladies had an important counterpart in the male gatherings called Academies. These were meetings of noble and upper class persons interested in intellectual discussion. A contemporary treatise, in fact, defines an academy as,

> an assembly of free and virtuous intellects, ready to look for knowledge with honest and friendly emulation; who under prescribed laws and statutes exert themselves in different honorable studies, now learning, now teaching, in order to become each day more virtuous and more wise.[22]

[22] Scipione Bargagli, *Della lodi dell' accademie...* (Florence, 1569), 13.

One of the more notable of these, the *Accademia Filarmonica* of Bologna, had a division for composers. To become a member, a composer submitted an *a cappella* composition of at least four voices, which was first examined by a special committee to determine if it were worthy. Next it was circulated among the composers who were already members and this was followed by an interview with the candidate during which questions about the composition could be asked. Finally, the question of admittance was voted on by the entire academy and if the candidate obtained a two thirds majority vote, he was admitted.[23]

[23] Ursula Brett, *Music and Ideas in Seventeenth Century Italy* (New York: Garland Publishing, 1989), 55.

Some of the private male academies made important musical contributions. One sponsored by the prince Ruspoli in Rome heard more than fifty cantatas by Handel and another hosted by cardinal Ottoboni frequently heard the trio sonatas by Corelli. A German visitor, J. F. A. von Uffenbach recorded his impressions of an oratorio performance in Ruspoli's palace in 1715, which is enlightening in its mix of aesthetic insight and aristocratic protocol.

> They performed a magnificent concert, or so-called oratorio, which so enraptured me that I was convinced that I had never heard anything of the kind so perfectly done before in my life ... Everyone listened so attentively to the excellent singers that not even a fly stirred except when a cardinal or a lady entered [while the music continued!], whereupon everyone stood, but afterwards sat down again in their former places ...

About halfway through the performance there was an interval during which large quantities of drinks, ices, cakes and coffee were brought in and offered to everyone. Then the second half of the work was given, and that altogether the performance lasted some four hours.[24]

One of the movements, which the intellectual discussions of the academies resulted in at the beginning of the eighteenth century, was a renewed fascination with the lives of the ancient Greeks, Romans and the period of the medieval crusades. Another was an interest in works dealing with Nature, of which the *Four Seasons* of Vivaldi is the most familiar today. Perhaps another manifestation of this interest were outdoor performances on noble estates, called "Serenatas," which were sometimes organized like elaborate Renaissance allegorical pageants, although on a smaller scale.

[24] Quoted in Malcolm Boyd, "Rome: the Power of Patronage," in *The Late Baroque Era* (Englewood Cliffs: Prentice Hall, 1994), 59.

6
On Civic and Military Music of the Italian Baroque

WHILE OPERA HAD BEGUN as a private entertainment of the aristocratic class, by the middle of the seventeenth century, scarcely fifty years later, opera was beginning to transform itself into an entertainment medium and a commercial business. Venice led the way in making such music available to the middle class in productions touring throughout Italy. There was still aristocratic support and money involved, however, and for the canon Cristoforo Ivanovich, it brought recollections of the use of mass entertainment for political control by the ancient Roman emperors.

> Abundance and display are the tools of delicate political operation, on which can depend the good fortunes of the government itself; through these, if used in honest measure, a prince can acquire the love of his people, by whom the yoke is never more easily forgotten than when they are sated or constrained by the pleasures. The common people, when they have nothing better to gnaw, turn to gnawing the reputation of princes; deprived of entertainment their idleness can easily degenerate, with the most dreadful of consequences …
>
> Public performances, since their introduction in Venice, have continued to take place every year during Carnival, thus setting an example which has come to be followed in many other parts of Europe.[1]

An important by-product of this transformation was the introduction of the repertoire principle. Purely private opera,

---

[1] Quoted in Lorenzo Bianconi, *Music in the Seventeenth Century*, trans. David Bryant (Cambridge: Cambridge University Press, 1987), 304.

like most music making throughout the eighteenth century, consisted of works written for only one performance. Once opera had become a commercial affair, the idea of sharing repertoire quickly occurred and by the end of the Baroque the same operas were being heard throughout Italy.

In Rome the concept of public opera had a more difficult path due to opposition from the Church, which since its very beginning had attacked theater for promoting sin. Now the Church was also bothered by its secular content and apparently by the idea of the public spending its money for such entertainment.[2] The Jesuit priest, Giovan Ottonelli, in a publication of 1652,[3] discussed some of the Church's concern, including the idea of an artistic medium devoted to profit and the use of female singers. Pope Innocent XII (1691–1700) even had an opera house in Rome torn down!

Nevertheless opera continued in Rome and where there is opera there must be opera teachers. A famous castrato, Giovanni Bontempi, has left a fascinating account of vocal study in Rome during the 1640s.

> The schools of Rome obliged their pupils to dedicate a total of one hour per day to the singing of difficult things; this served for the acquisition of experience. One hour on the trill, another on *passaggi,* a third on the study of letters, a fourth on training and other exercises—in the presence of the master and/or in front of the mirror—with the purpose of eliminating all unseemly movement of body, face, brows and mouth. These were the morning activities.
>
> After noon, pupils underwent half an hour of theoretical training, half an hour of counterpoint above a cantus firmus, an hour of instruction and practice in counterpoint in open score and a further hour in the study of letters; the remainder of the day was spent at the harpsichord or in the composition of some psalm, motet, canzonetta or other form of song, in accordance with individual flair and ability. These were the normal exercises for days on which pupils remained indoors.
>
> Outdoor exercises consisted of frequent trips to sing and listen to the echo outside Porta Angelica, with the aim of increasing self-criticism of the scholar's tone of voice; participation in almost all the music of the various churches of Rome; observation of the manners of performance of the many illustrious singers who flourished under Urban VIII; later,

[2] Malcolm Boyd, "Rome: the Power of Patronage," in *The Late Baroque Era* (Englewood Cliffs: Prentice Hall, 1994), 55.

[3] Giovan Ottonelli, *Cristiana moderazione del teatro* [1652].

at home, practice in these manners of singing and description thereof of the maestro: who himself, in his efforts to impress them more firmly upon the minds of the pupils, added all necessary warnings and other remarks. These exercises and general training in the art of music are those given us in Rome by Virgilio Mazzocchi, illustrious professor and maestro di capella of St. Peter's.[4]

[4] From *Historia musica* (Perugia, 1695), quoted in Bianconi, *Music in the Seventeenth Century*, 61.

In Venice and Naples forms of comic opera emerged as a popular medium attended by large crowds of paying citizens. It was for the Naples stage that the famous Pietro Metastasio (1698–1782) began his career. The Frenchman, Charles de Brosses, traveling in Italy in 1739, has left an account of hearing an opera in Naples which emphasizes the strong role of the public.

> This was the first grand opera that we had seen. The work by Sarri, a clever musician, but dry and sad, was not very good, but as a reward, was very well played. The famous Senesino played the main role; I was enchanted with the tastefulness of his singing and his bearing on the stage. But I felt with astonishment that the natives were not at all satisfied. They complained that he sang in a *stile antico.* I must tell you that musical taste changes here at least every ten years; all the applause was reserved for the Baratti woman, a new actress, pretty and easygoing, who was playing a man's part, a touching circumstance which perhaps contributed not a little to her getting such support ...
>
> An opera would not please at all if there were not, among other things, a pretended battle; one hundred rascals on both sides perform it, but they are careful to put in the first rows a certain number of swashbucklers who know how to handle weapons.[5]

[5] Charles de Brosses, "Lettres familieres ecrites en Italie en 1739," quoted in Carol MacClintock, *Readings in the History of Music in Performance* (Bloomington: Indiana University Press, 1979), 362ff.

Very little research has been done on the subject of civic wind band in this period of Italian history, but the names of such groups turn up in passing in various accounts. In Modena, one reads of a performance by three cornetti and five trombones, conducted by Paolo Bravusi, given in celebration of the visit of Isabella of Savoy in 1608.[6]

[6] Grove, *Dictionary* (1980), III, 221.

One reads of the *Cappella e del Concerto della Signoria* of Siena, whose leader, Alberto Gregori, was considered the first trombonist of Italy.[7] In Palermo a civic document of

[7] Alessandro Vessella, *La Banda* (Milan, 1935), 96.

1619 speaks of the trumpets and shawms [*pifari*] of the *musica di citta*.[8] A manuscript in Berlin, composed c. 1700 for the *Sonatori di fiato* by Francesco Magini, a professor at the conservatory of Rome, and the extant sonatas of Gussaghi (1608) dedicated to the "Excellent Virtuosi" of Venice, specifically the cornettist, Lodovico Cornale, also are testimonials to the presence of these civic bands.

[8] G. Di Marzo, *Diario della citta di Palermo*, II, 94.

The civic musicians for whom we have frequently quoted references are those from Bologna. One document pictures the civic trumpeters and the civic wind band escorting the city fathers.

> When they appear in public, these *Signori* are dressed in rich robes of silk, and during the winter they are muffled up with very precious furs as well. They are accompanied by a very respectable household of eight trumpeters, with a drummer, or player of the nakers, who with these trumpets play certain Moorish drums. To both the arms of liberty; also eight excellent musicians with trombones and cornetts ... [9]

[9] Vizani (1602), quoted in Don Smithers, *The Music and History of the Baroque Trumpet* (London: Dent), 77ff.

Another report speaks of the trombone and cornett ensemble performing concerts for the public from a balcony of the city hall as well as at the Church of St. Petronio.[10]

[10] Ibid.

> The main piazzas of the city are the great piazza, called the "Piazza del Comune," where the "Legato" and the governor and his "Auditori" live; also the "Gonfaloniere di Giustizia" with his "Signori Antiani"; There the city government meets, and the "Gonfalconieri del Popolo," and a company of Italian light cavalry. Above the door of this Palace is placed a very beautiful bronze statue of Pope Gregory XIII, who came from Bologna, which was made by the Bolognese smith, Alessandro Mengati ... and there is a very beautiful arch or balcony of stone, where trumpets are played every evening. And after the trumpets have finished, very pleasant music is played on trombones and cornettos at the same Piazza as well as the great building of the Church of St. Petronio.

By the seventeenth century the range of concert venues was beginning to expand. The jurist, Grazioso Uberti, in a book of 1630, mentions that concerts could be heard in "schools, private houses where concerts are given, palaces of princes, churches, oratories, open-air settings and the homes of composers."[11] We can assume there must have been much musical activity among the more prosperous merchant class in the major Italian cities, but virtually no research has concentrated on this facet of Baroque music. We have one insight relative to the German composer, Johann David Heinichen (1683–1729), who visited Venice in 1670 to study the Italian opera style. He became acquainted with the wealthy merchant, Bianchi, whose wife, Angioletta, was an active singer. There is one account of a performance which this family organized which included a work written by Heinichen. An eyewitness reported that this music,

[11] *Contrasto musico,* quoted in Bianconi, *Music in the Seventeenth Century,* 71.

> was performed from the water before the home of the merchant, which stood ... on the Grand Canal. Crowds of people gathered on the bridge and along the canal. As the first aria was sung, however, the clocks of the city began to strike, preventing the people from hearing. They began to indicate their vexation over this by stirring up such a loud noise that one could no longer hear the music. Madame Angioletta immediately asked them politely to be quiet to permit the music to continue. All became quiet again, though a repetition of the first aria was asked for, after which a tremendous cry of approval arose from the crowd; and the remainder of the serenade was received with no less approval.[12]

[12] J. A. Hiller, *Lebensbeschreibungen berümter Musikgelehrten und Tonkünstler* (Leipzig, 1784), 137.

A final manifestation of the growing public participation in music can be seen in an expanding market of publications of self-tutors for learning to play the violin and other instruments.

In an autobiographical poem by Antonio Abbatini, we have a first-hand description of one of the academies, which in this case, he tells us, met in his home. His description confirms other reports of these gatherings of upper class and noble gentlemen, for an evening with music and discussion of intellectual topics of the day.

> First, the now-lost madrigals of once upon a time
>   are, at table, sung with great delight:
>   the reason, for respect, I will not tell.

> There follows my address: I spread my wings
>   to raise myself to the harmonious skies;
>   but they are just like those of Icarus.
> Every liberty the virtuosi are allowed
>   to contradict whatever I have said,
>   though this role with reluctance do they play.
> Kircher has, however, always argued,
>   as, too, Orlandi, general of the Carmelites,
>   Dal Pane has his doubts, beloved Lelio too.
> Discussion over, as, by grace of God,
>   invariably occurs without ill-will,
>   due praise is then accorded he who most deserves.
> Here the unveiled truth is seen,
>   since almost all are in the fore-front row
>   and everything is discerned minutely.
> Then to the harpsichord the company transfers,
>   and each man takes upon himself to show, with song
>   and sound, his virtue, which binds the heart and soul.
> In all are set aside three hours of time,
>   from nine o'clock for the remainder of the day,
>   and never without wonder do those present go away.[13]

[13] Quoted in Lorenzo Bianconi, *Music in the Seventeenth Century*, 290ff.

Military Music

During most of the seventeenth century, military music in Italy seems to have consisted only of trumpets and timpani, belonging to units of civic militia as well as those attached to nobles.[14] In the civic militia of Rome, each military leader, *Capitano Generale,* had a personal ensemble of trumpets and drums. Such an example can be seen in Giovani Francesco Aldobrandini, with his four trumpets and *tamburo generale* during his campaign in Hungary in 1601. In addition, each company had two or more *tamburi* and sometimes a fife.[15]

During the seventeenth century, the cavalry, which was also divided into companies, had two or more trumpets in each and timpani were added in about 1650.[16] The dragoons, founded during the middle of the seventeenth century, had one tambour for each company of fifty to one hundred horses. Documentation from eighteenth century Naples indicates large numbers of fifes and drums. The Swiss guards in 1735 was organized into seven companies with eight

[14] Vessella, *La Banda*, 123ff.

[15] Ibid.

[16] Ibid.

fifes and fourteen tambours under a leader, growing by 1743 to nine fifes and twenty-nine drums for ten companies. The regiment of the royal Bourbon infantry in 1741 had six companies with fourteen tamburi and a *tamburo maggiore*.[17]

The first Hautboisten military band appears to have been brought to Italy from Paris by Vittorio Amadeo II when he married the niece to Louis XIV in 1684. At this time the name of his court wind band changes from *banda di trombone* to *banda di hautbois*.[18] In 1694 an additional small Hautboisten band was formed in the Guards to help with larger court celebrations, again an imitation of the French court.[19]

The first "oboe bands" appear in Rome in 1708 as *piccoli concerti*, consisting of oboes, bassoons and timpani, but appear to have been organized privately, independent of the civic government.[20]

At the end of the seventeenth century German influence begins to be seen in the Italian military bands, due to the presence of Austrian and German troops associated with the War of the Spanish Succession. When Charles II, King of Spain, died a semi-idiot in 1699, a will which had been extorted from him deeded the crown of Spain to the French Prince, Philip of Anjou, grandson to his sister, under the title of Philip V. However, according to the laws of hereditary descent, the crown should have gone to an Austrian, and so in Vienna the son of Leopold I was crowned King of Spain as Charles III. Thus the War of the Spanish Succession occurred, which made Italy one of the great battlefields for some fourteen years.[21]

Consequently one finds many names of German musicians in the military bands of this area, in particular Giorgio Cristoforo Albmeyer, who led the *Hautbois* of the Reggimento Rhebinder in around 1720–1722.[22] One finds additional military Hautboisten bands formed in the Reggimento di Piemonte (1737) and the Reggiment di Saluzzo (1750).[23]

[17] Ibid., 126.

[18] Ibid., 130ff.

[19] Ibid.

[20] Ibid., 123ff.

[21] John S. C. Abbott, *Italy* (New York, 1871), 473–474.

[22] Vessella, *La Banda*, 168.

[23] Ibid.

7
On Church Music of the Italian Baroque

THE GREATEST ACTIVITY in Italian Church related music occurred, of course, in the many churches of Rome, where also the Church sponsored educational institutions and the lay religious fraternities both sponsored a great deal of performance. The actual music for the service was retarded in development by the conscientious efforts of the popes to observe the dictates of the Council of Trent, which kept polyphony as the model, outlawed secular melodies and discouraged instrumental accompaniment and improvisation.

Things became temporarily more progressive under Pope Urban VIII (1623–1644), who loved music. He devoted more funds to music, including enlarging his choir, and appears to have been more tolerant of instrumental music, judging by some extant prints. Among these are the *Sacri armonici concentus* (1640) by Gregorius Urbanus, which contains independent instrumental works; the collection of *Masses* (1634) by Chinelli for voices and trombones; the *Messe a cinque* by Polidori, for five-part chorus, cornetti, trombones and organ; the *Pange lingua* by Bigaglia, for SATB chorus and three trombones and the eight *Cantate* for solo voice, oboe and *Flageoletto* by Torri. One chaplain, Nicolo Rubini, was also a famous cornettist, known as "Il Cavaliere del Cornetto," but his life was cut short by a murderer.

During this period, especially for special Church festival days, more modern forms such as concerti began to appear.

Andre Maugars, a violist and secretary attached to Cardinal Richelieu of Paris, was sent to Rome in 1639 on a diplomatic mission and reported back, "I have listened carefully to the most celebrated concerts in Rome." He has recorded one of the most interesting eyewitness accounts of the performance of church concerti in the manner of those described extensively in theory in Praetorius, *Syntagma Musicum*, III.

> To enable you to understand this distribution better, I will give you an example by describing to you the most celebrated and most excellent concert, which I heard at Rome the eve and the day of Saint Dominic at the church of the *Minerva*. This church is rather long and wide and there are two large elevated organs, one on each side of the main altar, where they had also placed two choirs. Along the nave there were eight other choirs, four on one side and four on the other, raised on platforms eight or nine feet high, an equal distance from one another and all facing one another. With each choir there was a portative organ, as is the custom. You must not be astonished, because one can find more than two hundred organs in Rome, while in Paris one could scarcely find two of the same tuning. The leading conductor beat the measure for the main choir, accompanied by the best voices. With each of the others there was a [sub-conductor] who did nothing but keep his eyes on the leading conductor, to conform his own beat to the leader's; in this way all the chorus sang in the same time, without dragging. The counterpoint was decorated, full of fine melodies, and many agreeable recitatives. Sometimes a high voice [*dessus*] in the first choir did a *recit*, then one of the 3rd, 4th, or 10th answered. Sometimes two, three or four voices from the different choirs sang together, sometimes the parts of all the choirs recited, each in turn, in emulation of each other. Sometimes two choirs contended with each other, then two others answered. Another time three, four and five solo voices sang together, and at the *Gloria Patri* all the choirs joined together. I must admit that I have never been so delighted; but especially in the Hymn and in the Prose, where ordinarily the conductor tries to do better, I heard singing that was perfectly beautiful: very elegant variety, very excellent inventions, and delightful different movements. In the Anthems they had also very lovely instrumental performances, with one, two, or three violins with the organ, and with archlutes playing certain dance tunes and answering each other.

> Let us place our hands, Sir, on our consciences and let us judge sincerely if we have similar performances; and even if we should have them, it seems to me that we do not at present have the voices; they would need a long period of performing together, whereas the Italian musicians never practice but sing all their parts at sight. And what I find more admirable is, that they never miss, though the music is very difficult, and that a voice in one choir often sings with the voice of another choir, which perhaps has never been seen or heard. What I beg you to notice is that they never sing the same Motets twice, though scarcely a day passes that there is not a festival in some church where some good music is played, so that one is assured every day of some new composition.[1]

Urban VIII also allowed secular elements associated with opera to become accepted in the form of large theater works focusing on the lives of the saints. These must have been as tedious as a sermon, for one of them, *Il palazzo incantato*, by Luigi Rossi, lasted eight hours in performance! One eyewitness to the changing style of Church music during the reign of Urban VIII was the nobleman, Vicenzo Giustiniani. The reader will especially notice his reference to the addition of improvisation in the old style [sixteenth century] polyphony.

> In the present course of our age music is not much in use, not being practiced in Rome by gentlemen, nor do they sing together with several voices as in past years, notwithstanding that it would provide the greatest possible opportunity to unify and sustain evening parties. Indeed, music is reduced to an unusual and almost new perfection, being practiced by a great number of good musicians who ... bring the greatest pleasure to whomever hears them by their artistic and sweet song. For having left the old style, which was somewhat unpolished, and also the excessive [improvisation] with which they embellished it, they now devote their attention for the most part to a recitative style, gracefully embellished with ornaments appropriate to the thought; and from time to time they execute passages with judgment and distinctness and with appropriate and varied consonances to mark the end of each period, in which the composers of today are wont to produce boredom with excessive and too frequent cadences. Above all, they make the words clear, using one note for each syllable; now piano, now forte, now slow, now fast—by the

[1] Andre Maugars, "Response faite a un curieux sur le Sentiment de la Musique d'Italie, Ecrite a Rome le premier Octobre 1639," quoted in Carol MacClintock, *Readings in the History of Music in Performance* (Bloomington: Indiana University Press, 1979), 118ff.

expression of their faces and by their gestures giving meaning to what they are singing, but with moderation and not in excess...

This style has even been introduced for the singing of Latin verses and hymns and odes of piety and devotion, sung with sweetness and great decorum, and so as to make the words and ideas clear and distinctly heard.

Today in compositions to be sung in church not so much value is given as formerly to the solidity and artistry of the counterpoint as to the great variety and diversity of the embellishments, and to the use of several choirs at solemn feasts with the accompaniment of orchestras of various instruments; even the recitative style is introduced. This music demands great practical knowledge and liveliness of invention and effort to write rather than great maturity and knowledge of refined counterpoint.[2]

[2] Vicenzo Giustiniani, *Discorso sopra la Musica* [c. 1628], trans. Carol MacClintock (American Institute of Musicology, 1962), 77.

We have another eyewitness report of one of these "recitative style" performances in Rome, by Andre Maugar a few years later.

There is still another kind of music which is not performed in France and which for this reason deserves my telling you about it separately. It is called *Stile recitativo*. The best that I have heard was in the Saint Marcel Chapel, where there is a congregation of the Brothers of the Holy Crucifix, composed of the greatest nobles of Rome, who as a consequence have the power to bring together every rarest thing in Italy; and, indeed, the most excellent composers seek the honor of having their compositions heard there, and try to present what is best in their studios.

This admirable and ravishing music is heard only on Fridays during Lent, from three to six o'clock. The church is not nearly as big as the Sainte Chapelle in Paris. At the end is a specious... screen with a medium-sized organ, very sweet and very suitable for voices. At the two sides of the church there are two small galleries where were located the best musical instruments. The voices began with a Psalm in the form of a Motet and then the instruments played a very good Sinfonia. The voices after this sang a story from the Old Testament in the form of a *comedie spirituelle*, like that of Susanna, of Judith and Holofernes, of David and Goliath. Each singer represented a personage of the story and perfectly expressed the energy of the words. Then one of its most celebrated preachers recited the Exhortation. When this was finished, the music recited the Evangel of the day, like the story of the Good Samaritan, the feast at Canaan, the story of Lazarus, of Mary Magdalen, of Our Lord's Passion, the singers imitating to perfection the personages of the Evangelist writes about. I cannot praise the Recitative Music enough; one must hear it to judge of its merit.[3]

[3] Andre Maugars, "Response faite a un curieux sur le Sentiment de la Musique d'Italie, Ecrite a Rome le premier Octobre 1639," 118ff.

Maugars has also left an interesting account of improvisation in Roman church music, which is particularly valuable for being a rare eyewitness report of the playing of the great Frescobaldi.

> As to the instrumental music, it was composed of an organ, a large clavecin, two or three violins, and two or three archlutes. At times a single violin sounded with the organ, and then another answered; another time all three played different parts together; and then all the instruments repeated together. Sometimes an archlute performed a thousand variations on ten or twelve notes, each variation five or six measures long; then another played the same passage differently, I remember one violin played purely chromatically, and though at first it seemed to me very hard on the ears, nevertheless I gradually grew accustomed to this manner and took great pleasure in it. But specially the great Frescobaldi brought out a thousand kinds of inventions on his clavier, the organ always holding firm.
>
> It is not without reason that this famous organist has acquired such a reputation in Europe; because his printed works render sufficient evidence of his skill, to judge his profound knowledge adequately you must hear him as he improvises toccatas full of refinement and admirable inventions. That is why he deserves that you hold him up as a unique player to all our organists, to make them want to come to hear him in Rome.[4]

[4] Ibid., 119ff.

The dogma and practice of Roman Church music had temporarily survived the humanists, but it found a more difficult challenge in the popularity of opera and the growing participation of the public in secular music in general during the sixteenth century. Whatever was the line between the influence of theatrical styles and the inclusion of actual secular music in the service, it was a line which seems to have been repeatedly crossed, as we see, for example, in the writings of Banchieri:

> The Masses, Psalms, Canticles, Motets and Concerti to be performed with the organ must be in the *affettuoso*, devout, attractive, and *recitativo* styles, imitating the words and employing gravity in concerting them.[5]

He particularly recommends in this regard the works of Viadana, in which "one, two and three voices sing in *stile recitativo*." One reference to theater style also reminds us that Italian terms such as "allegro" had earlier conveyed a style as well as a tempo.

> The *stile allegro* should not always be used, only at certain times; and also at the Elevation of the Holy Sacrament some serious sonata that moves one to devotion should be used.[6]

A visitor to Venice in 1709 reported,

> I do not know whether it is to cheer the Satans' days up even more and for the special satisfaction of those who only go to church as they go the the theaters, that they do scarcely ever fail in this noisy music to mingle the same that one has heard at the operas, and which have pleased more, and that with no scandal to the favor of the words which one changes and which, instead of expressing, for example, the loves of Pyramus and Thisbe, say something of the life of the saint whose feast day it is.[7]

The famous singing teacher, Tosi, was one who was particularly concerned with the secular styles he was hearing in the church.

> Since poor counterpoint has been condemned, in this corrupted age, to beg for a piece of bread in churches, while the ignorance of many exults on the stage, the most part of the composers have been prompted from avarice, or indigence, to abandon in such manner the true study, that one may foresee (in not succored by those few, that still gloriously sustain its dearest precepts) music, after having lost the name of science, and a companion of philosophy, will run the risk of being reputed unworthy to enter into the sacred temples, from the scandal given there, by their Jiggs, Minuets, and Furlanas;

[5] Adriano Banchieri, "Conclusioni nel suono dell' organo," quoted in Lorenzo Bianconi, *Music in the Seventeenth Century,* trans. David Bryant (Cambridge: Cambridge University Press, 1987). Banchieri (1567–1634) was a priest at the monastery S. Michele near Bologna, as well as a composer and organist.

[6] Ibid., 127.

[7] C. Freschot, *Nouvelle relation de Venise* (Utrecht, 1709), 318.

and, in fact, where the taste is so depraved, what would make the difference between the church music and the theatrical, if money were received at the church doors?[8]

......

[We must condemn] the presumption of a singer who gets the words of the most wanton airs of the theater rendered into Latin, in order to sing them with applause in the Church; as if there were no manner of difference between the style of one and the other; and, as if the scraps of the stage were fit to offer to the Deity.[9]

Marcello, in his satire, "Theater in the Modern Style" [1720] also mentions hearing disguised secular music in the church.

> The composer will have little facility in reading and still less in writing, and therefore will not understand Latin, even though he must compose church music, into which he will introduce sarabands, gigues, courantes, etc., calling them fugues, canons, double counterpoints, etc.[10]

Such performances stimulated the Church to issue a series of papal edicts, in 1657, 1662, 1678 and 1692. These were issued in an attempt to prevent secular influences from entering the service. In the "Edict on Music" of 1665, the pope demands that no words but the Latin in the Roman Missal be used and that the music be "grave, ecclesiastical and devout" in character.[11] The rather dark character of this attack can be seen in the following provisions.

> Eighth, that within a period of twenty days from the publication of the present edict by the Fathers Superior and others whose duty it is, that shutters or narrow grilles be placed in the choirs, be the latter temporary or permanent, and that the said shutters be of such a height as the singers will not be seen, under pain of privation of office and other penalties at the discretion of the Holy Visitation.
>
> Ninth, that no maestro di cappella or other person entrusted with ordering the music or giving the beat contravene the aforesaid prescriptions under pain of privation of office and perpetual disqualification from the exercise of this office and the right to make music; and, moreover, that he be punished with a fine of 100 scudi, of which one quarter be given

[8] P. F. Tosi, *Observations on the Florid Song* (London: Wilcox, 1743), VII, xxv.

[9] Ibid., IX, lxiv.

[10] Benedetto Marcello, "Il teatro alla moda," quoted in Oliver Strunk, *Source Readings in Music History* (New York: Norton, 1950), 525.

[11] The full text is quoted in Lorenzo Bianconi, *Music in the Seventeenth Century,* trans. David Bryant (Cambridge: Cambridge University Press, 1987), 108ff.

the denouncer (whose name will be held secret), three quarters to the holy places at the discretion of the Holy Visitation, and with other penalties—including corporal punishment—at the discretion of the said Holy Visitation.

During the early part of the seventeenth century, the most progressive Church music was heard in Venice at St. Mark's, where the great tradition of instrumental music begun at the end of the sixteenth century continued to develop. An eyewitness to some of these celebrations, Jean-Baptiste Duval, French ambassador to the Republic of Venice in 1607–1609, reported a procession on the eve of Ascension in 1608 with "eight standards, six silver trumpets and oboes."[12] A water procession on Easter Sunday, 1608, featured the galley of the doge, pulled by smaller boats containing oboe bands.

Duval also reported the use of winds during the actual Mass, in one case "different wind instruments were sounded, such as clarions, trumpets, oboes and drums."

An Englishman, Thomas Coryat, visiting in 1608, has left an account of the music he heard inside St. Mark's which lists both the older trombones and cornetts and one of the new strings.

> At that time I heard much good Musicke in Saint Markes Church, but especially that of a treble violl which was so excellent, that I thinke no man could surpasse it. Also there were sagbuts and cornets as at St. Laurence feast which yeeled passing good musicke.[13]

One sees reference here to another change in church music, the growing interest in string instruments. This change in taste, which brought to an end centuries of domination by winds in art music, was due in part to the advance in the quality of the manufacture of string instruments during the seventeenth century and in part because of the interest of the humanists in the ancient Greek accounts of singing accompanied by strings. Of the wind instruments, Agazzari notes,

> I shall say nothing, because they are not used in good and pleasing consorts, because of their insufficient union with the

[12] This and following descriptions are quoted in Egon Kenton, *Life and Works of Giovanni Gabrieli* (American Institute of Musicology, 1967), 35ff.

[13] Ibid., 37.

stringed instruments and because of the variation produced in them by the human breath, although they are introduced in great and noisy consorts.[14]

At the same time, during the seventeenth century the winds were going through a dramatic transformation of their own, with the retirement of nearly all the Renaissance instruments and their replacement by the modern instruments by 1675. Clearly a long period ensued during which makers struggled with improvements and players struggled with having to learn entirely new instruments, resulting in complaints about such things as intonation. A typical example is found in Charles Burney, who maintains he heard Alessandro Scarlatti say, "My son, you know I hate wind instruments, they are never in tune."[15]

Since Venice, and some Northern courts, had managed to preserve limited independence from the pope, some progress toward carrying the new ideas of the Baroque into church music occurred. Already in 1614 we can see in Alessandro Grandi, then working in Ferrara but soon to become *vicemaestro* to Monteverdi at St. Mark's, a desire to introduce the principles, if not the style, of the new opera into his motets. In the preface to this publication, Grandi makes both a subtle attack on the old, but official, polyphonic style and a subtle argument for something new.

> Here, the clarity of the words is not impaired by the fugues of the composer, nor is the art of speaking rendered any less excellent through the art of song; on the contrary, the latter is elevated and humbled, runs, rests and cries with the former; in whatever way the former is arranged, the latter gives rise to a more effective portrayal of the affections therein.[16]

Monteverdi refers to the tradition of winds supporting the voices in a letter of 1616 when he recommends this for a theatrical work as well.

> There are two more choruses . . . , but it seems to me that these ought to be doubled by wind instruments, for if they were performed in this way, what pleasure—I ask Your Lordship—would they not bring to the senses![17]

[14] Agostino Agazzari, "On Playing upon a Bass in . . . Consort," quoted in Oliver Strunk, *Source Readings in Music History* (New York: Norton, 1950), 425. One of his letters in 1606 speaks of the individual aesthetic characteristics of the lute, viols and violin.

[15] Quoted in Robert Donnington, *The Interpretation of Early Music* (New York, 1964), 548.

[16] Quoted in Bianconi, *Music in the Seventeenth Century*, 118.

[17] Letter to Alessandro Striggio (December 29, 1616), quoted in *The Letters of Claudio Monteverdi* (Cambridge: Cambridge University Press, 1980), 120.

A very large number of instrumental works, especially canzoni, were published at this time in Venice and records at the cathedral prove this music was performed during the service. In particular, between 1600 and 1620 many canzoni were published by such composers as Canale (1600), Mortaro (1600), Quagliati (1601), Bonelli (1602), Troilo (1606), Taeggio (1608), Rossi (1608), Bottaccio (1609), Bargnani (1611), Rovigo (1613), Bona (1614), Merula (1615), Lapi (1616), Picchi (1625), Marini (1629) and Frescobaldi (1628), in addition to collections of such works. Among the latter is the collection published by Rauerij (Venice, 1608), which includes some Gabrieli works found nowhere else and the Canzona for four instrumental choirs by Massaino.[18] For those who today know only the canzoni of Gabrieli, perhaps the above list will make the point that he, apart from his great quality, was also only the tip of the iceberg.

[18] This collection is available in a modern score from Leland Bartholomew, Music Department, Fort Hays State College, Fort Hays, Kansas.

This cathedral was also a great center for organ playing and the organists there were especially known for their improvisation. But even in Venice one could be too progressive. The officials of the cathedral in 1639 issued an edict warning that,

> in musical solemnities, the use of instruments other than those normally used in the church is not allowed; in particular, refrain from the use of warlike instruments such as trumpets, drums and the like, more suitable for armies than for the house of God ... and that all the musicians, secular and ecclesiastical alike, while serving their musical functions, must come dressed in surplices; and, finally, that the transposition of words or the singing of newly-invented words not contained in the holy books [are not] permitted except at Offertory, Elevation and after the Agnus Dei.

The lay religious fraternities in Venice were especially known for their private support of Church music. The French ambassador to the Republic of Venice in 1607–1609, Jean-Baptiste Duval, recorded seeing "six oboe players dressed in long robes with wide sleeves of dark blue or of rosy silk" representing the fraternity of St. Theodore in the annual Corpus Christi procession.[19]

[19] Ibid., 35ff.

These lay organizations also sponsored concerts of their own, the most documented of which were given at the Scuole San Rocco. Thomas Coryat describes a performance there on August 16, 1608, which included among its participants none other than Giovanni Gabrieli. Of particular interest is the description of a countertenor, who the writer could hardly believe was not a castrato.

> This feast consisted principally of Musicke, which was both vocall and instrumental, so good, and delectable, so rare, so admirable, so super-excellent, that it did even ravish and stupifie all those strangers that never heard the like. But how others were affected with it I know not; for mine own part I can say this, that I was for the time even rapt up with Saint Paul into the third heaven. Sometimes there sung sixeteen or twenty men together, having their master or moderator to keepe them in order; and when they sang, the instrumentall musitians played also. Sometimes sixeteene played together upon their instruments, ten Sagbuts, foure Cornetts, and two Viol-de-gambaes of a extraordinary greatness; sometimes tenne, six Sagbuts and foure Cornets; sometimes two, a Cornet and a treble violl. Of these treble viols I heard three severall there, whereof each was so good, especially one that I observed above the rest, that I never heard the like before. Those that played upon the treble viols, sung and played together, and sometimes two singular fellowes yeelded admirable sweet musicke, but so still that they could scarce be heard but by those that were very neare them. These two Theorbists concluded that nights musicke, which continued three whole hours at the least. For they beganne about five of the clocke, and ended not before eight. Also it continued as long in the morning: at every time that every severall musicke played, the Organs, whereof there are seven faire paire in that room, standing all in a rowe together, plaied with them. Of the singers there were three or foure so excellent that I think few or none in Christendome do excell them, especially one, who had such a peerless and (as I may in a manner say) such a supernaturall voice for such a privilege for the sweetness of his voice as sweetness, that I think there was never a better singer in all the world, insomuch that he did not onely give the most pleasant contentment that could be imagined, to all the hearers, but also did as it were astonish and amaze them. I alwaies thought that he was a Eunuch, which if he had beene, it had taken away some part of my admiration,

because they do most commonly sing passing well; but he was not, therefore it was much the more admirable. Againe it was the more worthy of admiration, because he was a middle-aged man, as about forty yeares old. For nature doth more commonly bestowe such singularitie of voice upon boyes and striplings, than upon men of such yeares. Besides it was farre the more excellent, because it was nothing forced, strained or affected, but came from him with the greatest facilitie that ever I heard. Truely, I thinke that had a Nightingale beene in the same roome, and contended with him for the superioritie, something perhaps he might excell him, because God hath granted that little birdie such a privilege for the sweetness of his voice, as to none other: but I thinke he could not much. To conclude, I attribute so much to this rare fellow for his singing, that I thinke the country where he was borne, may be proude for breeding so singular a person as Smyrna was of her Homer, Verona of her Catullus, or Mantua of Virgil. But exceeding happy may the Citie or towne, or person bee that possesseth this miracle of nature.[20]

[20] Quoted in Denis Arnold, "Music at the Scuola de San Rocco," *Music & Letters* 40, no. 3 (Jul., 1959): 236ff.

Unfortunately this great tradition gradually declined throughout the seventeenth century, owing to the increasingly conservative attitude of the Vatican. As a result, the brilliant instrumental forces heard in St. Mark's early in the century became the subdued music of string trios by the end of the century.

During the second half of the seventeenth century instrumental music began to flourish in both monasteries and convents, as well as in the *ospedali,* charitable institutions and schools for orphans, which in the case of those in Naples and Venice began to develop into early conservatories. We are fortunate to have eyewitness accounts of several of the individual *ospedali.* In 1698 the Russian, Petr Tolstago, wrote from Venice regarding the *Incurabili:*

In Venice there are convents where the women play the organ and other instruments and sing so wonderfully that nowhere else in the world could one find such sweet and harmonious song. Therefore people come to Venice from all parts with the wish to refresh themselves with these angelic songs, above all those of the Convent of the Incurables.[21]

[21] Quoted in W. Kolneder, *Antonio Vivaldi, his life and work* (London, 1756), 10ff.

A rather extraordinary account of another of these *ospedali,* that of the *Mendicanti,* is found in the *Confessions* of Jean-Jacques Rousseau, dating from two years after the death of Vivaldi.

> A kind of music to my mind far superior to that of the operas, and which has not its like in Italy is that of the *scuole* ... Every Sunday at the Church of each of these schools one has during Vespers motets for full choir and orchestra composed and directed by the greatest masters in Italy, performed in balconies with grilles, entirely by girls of whom the oldest is not twenty. I can imagine nothing so voluptuous, so touching as this music ... The church [the *Mendicanti*] was always full of those who liked this sort of music; even the actors from the Opera would come and conform themselves to the true taste in singing on these excellent models. What grieved me were those accursed grilles, which only allowed the sound to pass, and hid from me the angels of beauty of which the sound was worthy. I only talked of that. One day when I was talking about it to Monsieur le Blond:
>
> "If you are so curious," he said to me, "to see these little girls, it is easy to satisfy you. I am one of the administrators of the house; I want to give you tea there with them."
>
> I did not let him rest until he had kept his word to me. As we entered the salon which enclosed these such coveted beauties, I felt a shiver of love that I had never felt before. Monsieur le Blond introduced one after another to me of these famous singers whose voices and names were all known to me. "Come, Sophia ... " she was horrible. "Come, Cattina ... " she was blind in one eye. "Come, Bettina ... " smallpox had disfigured her. There was hardly one that did not have some notable defect. The executioner laughed at my cruel surprise ... I was grieved.[22]

[22] J. J. Rousseau, *Confessions*, II, vii.

Naturally we are most interested today in the *Seminario musicale dell' Ospitale della Pieta,* for it was there that the great Vivaldi was employed between 1704 and 1740. An account from early in Vivaldi's tenure records a visit by Frederick IV, King of Denmark and Norway.

> His Majesty made an appearance at the Pieta at eleven o'clock in the morning after hearing the embassy from the lords of Savoy, and the girls sang with the instruments of the maestro [Vivaldi] who occupies the podium in the absence of

Gasparini. Great was the applause for the *Credo* and *Agnus Dei* that were performed with the instruments, and then there was a concerto in great taste, as was appropriate.[23]

[23] Quoted in Remo Giazotto, *Antonio Vivaldi* (Turin, 1973), 105.

There is a curious reference to this *Ospitale,* and its musical activities, by a traveling Englishman in 1720. We can only speculate that it was to excite the English reader that he characterizes Vivaldi as a eunuch and the general environment more like a Turkish harem!

> There are in Venice four of these female hospitals ... the Incurabili, the Pieta, Ospitaletto and the Mendicanti ...
> Every Sunday and holiday there is a performance of music in the chapels of these hospitals, vocal and instrumental, performed by the young women of the place; who are set in a gallery above and are hid from any distinct view of those below by a lattice of iron-work. The organ parts, as well as those of the other instruments, are all performed by the young women. They have an eunuch for their master and he composes their music. Their performance is surprisingly good; and many excellent voices are among them.[24]

[24] Quoted in Marc Pincherle, "Vivaldi and the Ospitali of Venice," *The Musical Quarterly,* 24, no. 3 (Jul, 1938): 301.

Another interesting account, because it hints at the amorous activities for which the Italian Catholic institutions were known, is by K. L. von Poellnitz, who visited in 1729.

> I am in some doubt whether I should reckon the music of the Venetian churches in the number of its pleasures; but on the whole, I think I should, because certainly their churches are frequented more to please the ear, than for real devotion. The church of La Pieta which belongs to the nuns who know no other father but love, is most frequented. These nuns are entered very young, and are taught music, and to play on all sorts of instruments, in which some of them are excellent performers. Apollonia actually passes for the finest singer, and Anna-Maria for the first violin in Italy. The concourse of people to this church on Sundays and holidays is extraordinary. It is the rendezvous of all the coquettes in Venice, and such as are fond of intrigues have here both their hands and hearts full. Not many days after my arrival in this city I was at this very church, where was a vast audience, and the finest of music.[25]

[25] K. L. von Poellnitz, *Memoirs* (London, 1737), I, 414.

In 1739, just before Vivaldi retired from this service, another visitor recalled,

> The most transcendent music here is that provided by the Ospitali. There are four of these, all of them for girls—illegitimate, orphans, or those whose relatives are not able to care for them. They are being brought up at the expense of the state and are being trained most especially to excel in music. In addition they sing like angels, they play the violin, the flute, the organ, the clarinet, the violoncello, and the bassoon. In short, there is no instrument so large as to give them pause ... They are the sole performers at each concert, and some forty of them take part. I swear there is nothing more pleasing to be seen than one of these pretty young sisters in her white dress with a cluster of pomegranate blossoms over one ear, conducting an orchestra and beating time with all the grace and precision imaginable.[26]

[26] Quoted in Arnold, "Music at the Scuola de San Rocco," 301ff.

In this same year Charles de Brosses also mentions the quality of the orchestral performances.

> The one of the four *ospedali* I visit most often, and where I enjoy myself most, is the Ospedale della Pieta; it is also the first for the perfection of the symphonies. What strictness of execution! It is only there that one hears the first attack of the bow, so falsely vaunted at the Paris Opera.[27]

[27] Charles de Brosses, *Lettres familieres sur l'Italie* (Paris, 1931), I, 238ff.

It is generally understood that a great deal of Vivaldi's music, in particular the concerti, was composed for these students. Pincherle finds proof of this in the "extreme rapidity of composition, as evidenced by the autographs."[28] This facility in composition is evidenced by Vivaldi himself, as recalled by Charles de Brosses in 1739.

[28] Arnold, "Music at the Scuola de San Rocco," 310.

> Vivaldi has become one of my intimate friends, so as to sell me some very expensive concertos. He has in part succeeded, and I too in that which I desired, namely to hear him and have frequent good musical recreation: he is a *vecchio* with a prodigious fury for composition. I have heard him boast that he has composed a concerto, with all its parts, faster than a copyist could write it out.[29]

[29] Charles de Brosses, *Lettres familieres sur l'Italie*, I, 237ff.

Another extraordinary testimonial to the speed with which Vivaldi composed is found in the diary of J. F. von Uffenbach. On March 6, 1715, he writes,

After the meal, Vivaldi, the famous composer and violinist
came to my lodging, since I had sent to his house several
times to invite him. I spoke to him of some concerti grossi
that I would have liked to have from him, and ordered them
from him. Since he belonged to the circle of the Cantores I
had some bottles of wine brought, and he played some very
difficult improvisations for me on the violin, quite inimitable.
Close to I admired his art even more, and I realized from
the evidence that he played extraordinarily difficult and
varied things, but in a manner that was neither pleasant nor
cantabile.[30]

[30] Quoted in Alan Kendall, *Vivaldi* (London: Granada Publishing, 1979), 100.

Then, only three days later, we find this entry:

In the afternoon Vivaldi came to my lodging and brought, as
I had ordered from him, ten concerti grossi which he said he
had composed specially for me.

Ten concerti grosso in three days?! In any case, the assumption that many of the concerti were written for his students is clearly suggested in the duties outlined in his contract of 1735.

The same maestro will have to provide for our girls concertos
and other compositions for all sorts of instruments, and
he will have to come with the assiduousness necessary for
instructing the girls and making them well able to perform
them.[31]

[31] Archivio di Stato, Venice, Ospitali, busta 692, Notatorio Q, fol. 113r.

We might add that we find one indication of both the speed of composition and the educational purpose in such musical shorthand as the so-called "Alberti-bass" figures in upper melodic voices. In our view the "Alberti-bass" figure is nothing more than a chord symbol for the purpose of providing the chord for improvisation. The ear is the judge of this, as most performances of such passages as written sound ridiculous. An obvious example is the famous Vivaldi *Concerto* for Piccolo which is so often performed today. At the point the piccolo first enters, marked "Solo," the orchestra has nine bars with a C major chord on the first beat, followed by rests, in each bar. The following two bars consist also of only a C major chord. Thus, there is no "music" in the orchestral part, only grammar. What is the solo doing? The piccolo has only "Alberti-bass" figures. Thus there is no "music" in the solo part, only grammar. Question: Where is the music? Can anyone really believe that Vivaldi really wanted the listener to hear eleven bars of something so musically stupid? If the soloist does not improvise, there is no music—only grammar.

We beg all musicians: in the music of the Baroque, please do not ever again play "Alberti-bass" figures.

8
Thoughts on Music of the Spanish Baroque

THE REMARKABLE PERIOD which began with the marriage of Ferdinand of Aragon to Isabella of Castile in 1469 had included the acquisition of Granada from the Moors (1492), Navarre from the French (1515) and of course the vast new colonial empire resulting from the discovery of America. Poor management, of both economic and political resources, brought about the decline which is symbolized by the defeat of the Armada in 1588.

With the death of Philip II in 1598 the fortunes of Spain began to decline even faster, due to several economic conditions. The administration of the colonies had become increasingly costly and the plunder of gold and silver was no longer covering the costs of empire. The defeat of the armada made attempts to maintain sea trade more expensive. Inflation was rampant and the population base was declining due to emigration.

During the seventeenth century Spain's land holdings made it the greatest empire in the world. Unfortunately, the genetic wheel of fortune, the central problem in dynastic government, left Spain with no men capable of fulfilling the potential of this rich empire. For example, Philip III (1598–1621) was a weak man incapable of governing, who turned the responsibility of government over to Francisco Gomez de Sandoval y Rojas, Duke of Lerma. The latter not only drained the treasury, but ruthlessly expelled 400,000 Christian Moors to Africa in order to confiscate their property.

The reader will understand that this political and economical atmosphere did not create an atmosphere for the nurture of great music and music making. In addition, Spain had become, under Isabella "the Catholic," a country more Catholic than Italy. As such, it is no surprise that the resident philosophers repeated the old dogmas of past Church history. Baltasar Gracian, for example, reflects the Church's long-held dogma that man must be ruled by Reason.

> It is an outstanding sign of wisdom to keep a cool head during fits of rage: all extremes of feeling are a falling away from reason.[1]

On the other hand, Grecian recognized that some people are simply different and are motivated other than by Reason.

> In some the heart reigns, in others the head. Is there anything more foolish than to use courage to study and wit to fight?[2]
> ......
> Some people excel at quick thinking, others at quick doing. The former please, the latter astonish.[3]

Gracian also reflected the teachings of the Church in his references to the emotions. The Church had long regarded emotions as the gateway to sin. Thus, as Gracian echoes, man's salvation lies in overcoming them.

> A man who is not passion's slave reveals the highest quality of soul; his superiority itself redeems him from subjection to passing, vulgar influences. There is no greater mastery than control over oneself and one's emotions; it comes to be a triumph for a man's free will.[4]

He also attempts to connect this with art, observing,

> Art would be deficient if it merely taught you to conceal the limits of your talent. It must also teach you to disguise the impetus of your emotions ...
> Discovering someone's emotions is like opening a breach in the fortress of his talent.[5]

In another place, he gives a variant of this last sentence:

---

[1] Baltasar Gracian, *The Oracle,* Nr. 155, trans. L. B. Walton (London: Dent, 1953). Gracian (1601–1658) was educated at Toledo and became a member of the Society of Jesus in 1619. Although he continued his works as a priest for some time, by 1640 he was well-known in literary circles.

[2] Baltasar Gracian, *A Pocket Mirror for Heroes,* trans. Christopher Maurer (New York: Currency Doubleday, 1996), 29.

[3] Ibid., 157.

[4] Gracian, *The Oracle,* Nr. 8.

[5] Gracian, *A Pocket Mirror for Heroes,* 7.

> The emotions are the breaches in the defenses of the mind.[6]

[6] Gracian, *The Oracle*, Nr. 98.

Such an attitude, of course, is completely opposed to the basic nature of music.

The Church had also long held the sense of sight in special distinction among the senses. Few philosophers after the Middle Ages discussed the senses much, but we thought the reader might enjoy a discussion by Gracian on why we don't have *earlids*. The reader will also notice here the reference to sounds being of such brief duration, the basis of much questioning of the virtue of music in medieval literature. It is also interesting here to read Gracian's observation about the ability of hearing to process information at a greater speed than speech—an harbinger of the variable-speed tape recorder.

> We have eyelids but not earlids, for the ears are the portals of learning, and Nature wanted to keep them wide open ... The ears hold court at all hours, even when the soul retires to its chambers. In fact, it is then that those sentinels ought to be most wide awake. If not, who would warn of danger? When the mind goes lazily off to sleep, who else would rouse it? This is the difference between seeing and hearing. For the eyes seek out things deliberately, when and if they want, but things come spontaneously to the ears. Visible things tend to remain: if we don't look at them now, we can do so later; but most sounds pass by quickly, and we must grab that opportunity by the forelock. Our one tongue is twice enclosed, and our two ears are twice open, so that we can hear twice as much as we speak.[7]

[7] Gracian, *A Pocket Mirror for Heroes*, 87ff.

In discussing art in general, Gracian begins with an interesting quotation of Michelangelo:

> Self-satisfaction is the beatitude of the simple. "Lucky you," Michelangelo once said, "who are content with your vile doodlings while I get no satisfaction from anything I paint."[8]

[8] Ibid., 92ff.

Gracian is considerably more decided when it comes to the value and purpose of art, however.

> Man is born a barbarian; he is saved from being a beast by acquiring culture. Culture, therefore, makes the man, and

the greater his culture the greater the individual. By virtue of her culture, Greece was in a position to call the rest of the world barbarous. Ignorance is most uncouth; nothing refines so much as knowledge.[9]

......

Art. She, too, is an enchantress. But whereas Circe changed men into pigs, Art changes beasts into people.[10]

No doubt because of the same conditions which limited the production of important music and performance in Baroque Spain, there is relatively little important discussion of music in the seventeenth century Spanish literature. An occasional interesting use of music as a metaphor reminds us that music was in fact a conversant topic in society. In his poem, the "First Solitude," Gongora creates a nice metaphor of "weaving their voices in alternate song" to represent the moving of tree branches.[11] Quevedo, in his "The Dream of Death," used the expression "no one sings well on an empty stomach" to mean a person should not speak if he has only something stupid to contribute to the conversation.[12]

Gracian returned to the familiar Platonic association of the well-adjusted human body with harmony:

> The divine philosopher was right to compare the human body to a resonant, living instrument. When it is well tuned, it makes marvelous music; and when it is not, it is all confusion and dissonance. It is composed of many, very different strings, incredibly hard to adjust to one another, and its pegs are always slipping. Some have called the tongue hardest to tune.[13]

One of the mirrors of seventeenth century Spanish life available to us is found in the dramatic works, since most playwrights now had begun to attempt to imitate real life to some degree. In this regard, it is interesting that, while the ability to soothe had always been a valued purpose of music, in seventeenth century Spain this subject appears to receive unusual emphasis in the plays. One is tempted to conclude that there was, among the educated class, a certain melancholy residual to the rapidly declining fortunes of the empire. In Molina's Old Testament play, *Tamar's Revenge* (I, lines 320ff), Tamar requests music.

---

[9] Gracian, *The Oracle*, Nr. 87.

[10] Gracian, *A Pocket Mirror for Heroes*, 60.

[11] Gongora, "First Solitude," lines 540, in Gilbert Cunningham, *The Solitudes of Gongora* (Baltimore: Johns Hopkins Press, 1964). Gongora (1561–1627) was born of noble parents and educated at a Jesuit lower school and at the University of Salamanca. In 1617 he was ordained as a priest in Madrid.

[12] Francisco de Quevedo, *Dreams and Discourses*, trans. R. K. Britton (Warminster: Aris & Phillips, 1989), 307.

[13] Gracian, *A Pocket Mirror for Heroes*, 86.

TAMAR. Oh, Dina, I am sick at heart.
DINA. It gives respite to my sadness
    when I start to sing.
TAMAR. In that case,
    give me your instrument to play ...
    Music was made to soothe our care.

Tamar then sings a song which begins,

My wanton thoughts of love
like a bird of hope that sings ...

In the meantime, Amnon has entered the stage and reacts as a contemplative listener to Tamar's song.

How gently, how passionately
she laments! How soft her voice!
Heavens, what bewitchment is this?
The very wind returns again
shamed by her mellifluous song—
and ashamed he might be
for being becalmed so long.
To serve as her accompaniment
he employs her voice to tune
his instruments; high pitched treble
of these leaves, bass of babbling streams ... [14]
I could listen for days on end
to you, without a wink of sleep.

[14] The sound of water running over stones is a frequent suggestion in lyric poetry for the invention of music in more than one part.

In Valdivielso's *The Bandit Queen* we find a similar reference to the purpose of music to soothe.

BANDIT QUEEN. Where are my musicians?
MUSICIANS [within]. Here we are, milady.
BANDIT QUEEN. Play me a song to divert me a while;
    When I think of treacherous Delight
    I feel so melancholy.

Molina's *Damned for Despair* (III, iii) offers this same purpose in the music of nature. The hermit Paulo who is walking in the woods to seek solace and addresses the birds,

Little songbirds,
innocent flatterers,
untaught musicians, idlers

among reed-beds and wild thyme,
cheer my sad spirits
with your melodies;
with your gentle voices
help me rise above my cares.

Twice in Calderon's *The Surgeon of Honor* reference is made to the ability of music to soothe and bring gladness, first in Act III:

DIEGO. Let's listen to the music in the street.
KING. We'll hear them sing awhile. Perhaps
    Their songs will help relieve my sadness.
DIEGO. Perhaps, your majesty. It's said
    That music is a source of gladness.

Also in Act III, the shepherd, Tirso, makes a remarkable reference to the ability of music to soothe.

Well, whatever it is, by God,
We'll sing a little song for you
and drive away your sorrows.
There's nothing else that's worth a damn.

A very unusual reference of the purpose of music to soothe is found in Calderon's *The Constant Prince* (I, i) when a lady of the court of the King of Fez finds it soothing to hear the sad songs of the Christian captives.[15] The following dialog is between the captives and two attendants of the lady.

FIRST CAPTIVE. Can Music, whose strange instrument
    Was our clanking gyves and chains—
    Can it be, our wail could bring
    Joy into her heart? Our woe
    Be to her delight?
ZARA. It's so;
    On this account she'll hear you; sing.
SECOND CAPTIVE. Ah! these sufferings exceed,
    Lovely Zara, all the rest,
    Since from out a captive's breast
    (Save a soulless bird's indeed)
    Never has a willing strain
    Of music burst.
ZARA. But have not you

[15] In II, ii, four lines of lyrics for a captive Christian song is given.

        Yourself sung many a time?
THIRD CAPTIVE. It's true;
        But then it was no stranger's pain
        To which we hoped at last to bring
        Some ease. It was our own sharp grief
        For which in song we sought relief.
ZARA. She is listening now. Then sing.
CAPTIVES [sing]. *Age does not respect*
        The fair or the sublime;
        Nothing stands erect
        Before the face of time.
ROSA. Captives, you can now retire,
        And your pleasant concert end.

In one instance, the listener's feelings are such that he doubts that even music can soothe them. In Molina's *Tamar's Revenge* (II, lines 170ff), we find,

AMNON. What's that noise? Ho, there! Who's singing?
JONADAB. The musicians that you summoned,
        my good lord, to alleviate
        with their harmonies the blackness
        of your melancholy humor.
AMNON. Well tell them they're wasting their breath.

Similarly, in Calderon's *Life is a Dream* (II, i), shortly after a stage direction calls for "music and song," and perhaps reflecting on Spain's past period of military glory, a character can be soothed not by ordinary music, but by only the sound of the soldiers song.

FIRST SERVANT. May they sing again?
SIGISMUND. No, no;
        I don't care to hear them sing.
SECOND SERVANT. I conceived the song might bring
        Some ease to your thought.
SIGISMUND. Not so;
        Sounds that only charm the ear
        Cannot soothe my sorrow's pain;
        It's the soldier's martial strain
        That alone I love to hear.

The deep spiritual roots of Spanish society are evidenced in two instances in seventeenth century plays where the purpose of music is for prophesy. In Calderon's *The Surgeon of Honor* (Act III) there is a group of musicians who sing songs of prophesy, and in Molina's *The Trickster of Seville* (III) songs of prophesy are sung by off-stage singers from the spirit world who accompany the "Stone Guest."[16]

[16] This play is one of the sources for Mozart's *Don Giovanni*.

Finally, these plays include two interesting references to serenades. In Calderon's *The Painter of his Dishonor* (II, lines 1622), there is a serenade with a very rare reference to a singer accompanying himself on a harp. It is also rare to find the suggestion that it would be the quality of the music, rather than the quality of the singing or the young man, which would determine the young lady's response. The Prince warns,

> Listen carefully;
> Depending on the tune, she'll tell me either
> To approach the balcony or to retire.

In Molina's *The Trickster of Seville* (Act I, lines 451ff) a peasant girl gives a remarkable explanation, together with timeless observations, for her tendency to be unmoved by the love songs of a young man.

> Sometimes as well he'll offer me sweet music,
> The soft guitar, the shepherd's gentle flute,
> Their music dedicated just to me.
> Despite all this, I'm totally unmoved,
> For I am ever mistress of my fate,
> As far as love's concerned, it's queen and sovereign.
> In fact, my greatest pleasure is his pain,
> And in his suffering I find my heaven.
> The other girls willingly die for him,
> While I, at every opportunity,
> Destroy his eager hopes with my disdain;
> But isn't this the proper thing to do
> In love's affairs? To love the man who hates
> You; likewise, to despise the man who loves?
> For if you favor him, you'll kill his love;
> Despise him and he'll love you all the more.

We turn now to reflections of the music of the aristocrats of the Spanish Baroque, but first, in a comment by Gracian, we see that as in England the nobles are no longer participating in performance themselves.

> Not all arts deserve esteem, nor all occupations. To know everything is no grounds for criticism, but *practice* everything and your good name will suffer ... Philip II of Spain chided his son for singing in his chamber.[17]

[17] Gracian, *A Pocket Mirror for Heroes*, 20ff.

And so it was that Spanish music in the seventeenth century suffered from the great separation between the aristocracy and the middle and lower classes. Most composers and professional musicians were forced to earn a living as servants to the court and little art music seemed to trickle down. Thus, while the publication of music was expanding enormously in Northern Europe, there was very little such activity in Spain. At the same time there appears to have been little foreign enlightenment. Although there were many foreign instrumentalists at court, their influence in bringing any of the exciting new developments from the North is difficult to document. Even the craze for Italian music which was capturing the rest of Europe only becomes a significant factor in Spain at the end of the century.

One contemporary insight into the slow development of Spanish music is offered by Domenico Cerone, who, although an Italian, wrote the first important book on music in the Spanish language, the *El Melopeo y Maestro* (1613).[18] In Book I, Chapter LIII, he offers several reasons why he finds Spanish musical development lagging behind the Italians. He finds the Spanish "masters" not as diligent, the teachers lacking in patience and the composers simply not writing much music. He also reports that he knew no academies for music in Spain, except for a private one sponsored by the Austrian wife of Philip II. Finally, Cerone reports that due to the strong religious roots in Spain, nearly all musical energy was devoted to the improvement of church music. Indeed, in his own book of some 1,200 pages, there is not a single illustration of instrumental music, nor any biographical information on important Spanish instrumentalists.

[18] Book 22 contains a number of "enigma" canons, in the form of a cross, a key, a sword, etc., as well as one resolvable by throwing dice.

The music favored by the court of Philip III was entertainment music, beginning with allegorical forms in the tradition of the sixteenth century. The private entertainment of the king centered on dancing, for which the court string players devoted much of their time. Cerone notes that while the king paid his musicians unusually high salaries, few other nobles were personally active in support of music at this time. The nobles were, however, quick to engage the necessary musicians to add to their luster in public appearances, as we see in an eyewitness description of a procession in Madrid in 1623.

> The honourable TOWNE of Madrid sent forth foure trumpets on horseback, with caparisons of orange-coloured taffats laid with silver lace, and the Trumpeters in cassocks of the same, blacke hats lined with orange-coloured taffeta, orange-coloured plumes and silver furniture ...
>
> There followed the Townetroope, foure Trumpets of the Lord DON DUARTE in a liverie of tawny taffeta, with gabardines layd with silver lace, and hats of the same, with tucks of silver, tawny plumes, and brances of silver ...
>
> It was requisite the Duke of Infantado should follow ... He brought with him foure Trumpeters in white freezado mantles, with gabbberdines of blacke damaske, edged with silver lace ...
>
> Presently there entered the ADMIRALL of CASTILLE's troup ... There went before his horse foure Trumpetters in long coates of balcke satin, garded with gold lace ...
>
> Four trumpets of the Count de Monterey followed, with long coates of white satin, lacaes and flowers of gold, hats of the same, blacke plumes and golden furniture ...
>
> Don Francisco de Sandoval y Roias ... brought four trumpets in four freezado coates, clad in gabberdines of blue satin, laid with silver lace, blacke hats, wreathes and bands of silver, blue plumes ...
>
> The horse were all in number 523, with those of the Trumpets, Kettle-drummes ... [19]

Philip IV (1621–1665) was also little interested in government, turning over these mundane details to a cardinal, the Count of Oliveres. The cardinal involved himself in international intrigue and by 1642 had left Spain so weak that she was soon forced to give up the Netherlands and sign the Peace of the Pyrenees, which promoted the ascendancy of

[19] Nichols, *The Progresses of King James The First* (London, 1828), 892.

France. Meanwhile, the king lived a life of pleasure, which included strong support of art, poetry and the theater.

Philip was not so interested in music and between 1652 and 1655 made retrenchments in the court wind players in Madrid. No longer able to afford the importation of foreign musicians, the court ordered the leader of the court wind players, Francesco de Baldes (or, perhaps, Valdes) to organize a school for minstrels so the court would not be dependent on hiring foreign players. An extant document[20] reveals that he formed a band of twelve wind instruments, four soprano shawms, two tenor shawms, two "contra altos de shawm" and four trombones, which appears to be in imitation of the *Les Grands Hautbois* of Louis XIV in France.

[20] Edmond Vander Straeten, *La Musique aux Pays-Bas* (New York, 1969), VII, 436ff.

Charles II (1665–1700) was a lame, epileptic, senile half-wit, whom it was impossible to educate. He presided over the final collapse of the economy of the middle and lower classes, while the aristocracy continued in blind extravagance. Following the economic decline, there was a decline in the teaching of music and by the period of Charles II sufficient competent native singers could not be found to fill the openings in the royal chapel.[21] At the urging of the pope, Charles made his heir Philip, Duke of Anjoy, and for all practical purposes gave Spain to France.

[21] Louise K. Stein, "The Iberian Peninsula," in *The Late Baroque Era* (Englewood Cliffs: Prentice Hall, 1994), 413.

After the turn of the eighteenth century, following the marriage of Philip V to Maria Luisa of Savoy, French musicians began to play an important role in court music. Some important Italian musicians also began to arrive in Spain at this time, notably Domenico Scarlatti and the famous singer, Farinelli. Scarlatti followed his student, Princess Maria Barbara de Braganza to Spain when she married Ferdinand and his only duty seems to have been to produce sonata after sonata.

The influence of Italian style in Spain was not without protest. In particular the Benedictine Benito Feijo complained that the Italian music was noisy and lacking in traditional Spanish gravity. He objected that the Spanish had become slaves to a foreign taste. He particularly found the Italian use of harmony to be disturbing. "Harmony," he sighed, "becomes exasperating."[22]

The literature on the Spanish nobles of the Baroque includes little comment on military music. We can only find a few reflections in the stage plays. Perhaps the most familiar form of military music for contemporaries was the call to battle, as in Calderon's *The Constant Prince* (I, iii).[23]

> *Trumpets resound from within*
>
> FERNANDO. But what trumpet's this, whose sound
>   So disturbs the air and echoes from the ground?
>
> *Drums from the opposite side*
>
>   And in this direction too
>   Drums are heard, the music of the two
>   Is that of Mars.

Specific military signals for drums are found in Calderon's *Life is a Dream* (III, i), where there is a "sound to arms" and in *The Mayor of Zalamea* (I, xviii),

> Ho, drummer! Beat the call for all
> The troops to go to bivouac.

In Calderon's *The Mayor of Zalamea* (I, ii) we find lyrics for a genuine soldier's marching song. Just before the song a soldier gives the purpose of this music as being to "lighten our up-hill-and-down-dale march." And in his *The Mayor of Zalamea* (II, xix) the title of a military popular song is given, "A soldier's love lasts not a single hour."

The exclusive control of Spain by the aristocracy and the Church created a conservative atmosphere in which the sixteenth century Church styles continued on through much of the seventeenth century. Only the arrival of the vernacular, but sacred, *villancico* offered something truly contemporary to the broad public.

None the less, some churches continued to employ large numbers of wind instruments, who were probably used primarily in the performance of large church concerti. In the cathedral in Granada in 1563 one found six wind players in regular daily service, performing on flutes, cornetts,

---

[22] Quoted in Ibid., 426.

[23] In Calderon's *The Constant Prince* (III, iii) the stage direction calls for military trumpet signals. In his *Life is a Dream* (II, i), Clarin observes,

> For there are two things, I
>   believe,
> That are bad at keeping
>   secrets,
> A brass clarion and a lackey.

shawms, bassoons, horns, trumpets and trombones. During the seventeenth century cornets, oboes and horns were added to these instruments. The bassoon at this time became an indispensable part of the realization of the keyboard part.[24]

In the royal chapel in Toledo, the pastoral chants were accompanied by two shawms, a small "bassoon-serpentine" and bassoon.[25] There are also extant three *Masses* by Francisco Soler (1625–1688), composed for voices and wind band.[26] In Portugal, during the seventeenth century, cornetts, sackbuts and bassoons regularly accompanied the singers in the Badajoz Cathedral.[27]

No extant written information can help us recreate the original effect of the music for a religious service in Calderon's *Love after Death* (II, ii). First, there is a stage direction which mentions only "a crowd of Moors and musicians seen at a little distance." A very short time later another stage direction reads "The instruments continue to play during the remainder of this scene, which is intended to be performed in a ritualistic manner." Aside from the very rare instance at this time of music playing continuously underneath the dialog, we wish we could know what was meant by this "ritualistic" music. One can only judge from the dialog which follows:

> MALECA. What a strong and mournful feeling
>   This strange song awakens now!
> TUZANI. At this voice terror is stealing
>   Through my breast, I know not how!

Religious music is also called for in Calderon's *The Great Theater of the World*, which concludes with a joyous, musical celebration of communion.

> AUTHOR. The angels in heaven, and men on earth, hell's very demons, even, low kneel before this sacred Bread; now let the joyful sounds of earth, hell, heaven this Bread proclaim in sweet harmonious concord resonant. Let joyful pipes sing out their hymns.

This is followed by a stage direction reading,

[24] Grove, *Dictionary of Music* (1980), VII, 627.

[25] Vander Straeten, *La Musique aux Pays-Bas*, VIII, 194ff.

[26] Copies in E-Bc and E-G.

[27] Grove, IV, 817.

Sound of hornpipes is heard.
The Tantum Ergo is sung many times.

If anything, there seemed to be a greater enthusiasm for church music in Spanish Mexico. Torquemada, writing in 1615, found singers proficient in polyphonic music in every town of a hundred or larger and "competent instrumentalists are also found everywhere."[28] An Englishman in 1625 concluded the people were drawn to the churches "more for the delight of the music than for any delight in the service of God."[29]

In Puebla, the second largest city in seventeenth century Mexico, the cathedral used recorders, shawms, cornetts, sackbuts and bassoons to double, or even replace the voices. Violins do not appear until the eighteenth century. Surviving documents indicate that one of the leading composers, Juan Gutierrez de Padilla, maintained a shop in his home in which salaried workers produced "ecclesiastical instruments," bassoons, shawms and recorders.[30]

In Mexico City, the most important composer of the cathedral, Antonio de Salazar (1650–1715), set to music a poem by Juana Ines de la Cruz, which speaks of the typical church ensemble as being "clarino, trumpet, cornett, trombone, bassoon, and organ."[31]

We conclude these brief comments on Church music with a charming and humorous passage by Quevedo in his picaresque novel, *Buscon*,[32] which concerns the travels of Pablos, a comic anti-hero, presents an extensive satire of poets and poetry. First, on his way to Madrid, Pablos encounters an old priest riding a mule who complains that after years of submitting his poetry in "public contests for songs and carols for Corpus Christi and Christmas" he has never been awarded the prize. As an example of one of his unappreciated sacred songs he offers the following, which, of course, consists of all the wrong emotions for the occasion.

Shepherds, is it not great fun to say
Today's Saint Corpus Christi's day?
This is a day of joyous dances
When the tiny lamb so young

---

[28] Juan de Torquemada, *Monarqu'a indiana*, quoted in Steven Barwick, "Mexico," in *The Early Baroque Era* (Englewood Cliffs: Prentice Hall, 1994), 352.

[29] Ibid., 355.

[30] Grove, *Dictionary*, XV, 441 and XIV, 76.

[31] Ibid., XVI, 412.

[32] Francisco de Quevedo, *The Scavenger*, trans. Hugh Harter (New York: Las Americas Publishing Company, 1962), 66ff.

Shall hear his timely mourning sung ...
So sound away the gay sackbut
And lead us on our happy way.

Among the other works by this neglected poet was an epic describing 11,000 virgins, with fifty verses for each, and a comedy called *Noah's Ark*, in which the characters were cocks, rats, donkeys and wild boars. Only when he had finished the play, did he realize it could never be produced, since animals can't speak. When the poet also mentioned 900 sonnets for the "woman I love," Pablos asks about his personal experience in this regard and the poet responded that, as a clergyman, the sonnets were written in the spirit of prophecy.

When Pablos arrived in Madrid, reflecting on this poet as one of "those lunatics who live off poor wretches," he expressed his feelings by writing a proclamation against poets.

*Proclamation against addle-brained,
insipid and tasteless poets*

Being cognizant of the fact that this species of vermin known as poets are our neighbors and Christians, though bad ones; seeing that throughout the year they worship eyebrows, teeth, ribbons, and slippers, and commit other more grievous sins, we hereby ordain that during Holy Week, all publicly known and street-corner poets be gathered together as is done with bad women, and they be informed of their erroneous ways and be converted. To this end, we do hereby set aside houses for repentant poets ...

Furthermore, due to the fact that the devilish sect of men condemned to write poetry of perpetual concepts, splitters of words and perverters of reason, has infected our womenfolk with the disease of poetry, we do hereby declare ourselves revenged through the evil we have done to the latter for what the first female did to us through Adam. Because of the poverty and want that infects the globe, we order that all the couplets of the poets be burned like old trimmings, so as to extract the gold, silver and pearls, since in most verses the ladies are fashioned from all sorts of precious things, like statues with feet of clay ...

Furthermore, having observed that since many poets have ceased to write Moorish ballads—although they still preserve certain remnants of them—they have turned to pastoral verse, and that, as a consequence, the cattle are thin from imbibing their tears, scorched in the flames of their loves, and so enraptured with the sound of their music that they no longer graze, we do ordain that poets shall leave that occupation, and that those who are friends of solitude shall become hermits, and the rest—since it is lively work and abounding in obscene expressions—shall devote themselves to mule tending ...

Furthermore, noting the great harvest of quatrains, songs, and sonnets that have appeared during these fertile poetry years, we do ordain that all bundles of these poems which are found unsuitable for use as wrapping paper in the grocers' shops, be shipped off to the privies without further ado ...

But observing in our mercy that there exist in our land three types of people so terribly wretched that they can't live without poets, that is to say, actors, blind men and the clergy, we do ordain, therefore, that a few poets shall be permitted to profess their art, provided they obtain a license from the official censor of their home town ...

In conclusion, we do ordain that all poets in general stop their use of Jupiter, Venus, Apollo, and other gods, under pain of having to take these pagans for lawyers on their Judgment Day.

Later, however, Pablos himself becomes a poet. He becomes interested in writing plays, having discovered,

I was very much surprised to learn that dramatists are found among actors, for I had always thought they were intelligent and well-educated men and not people with so little culture.[33]

[33] Ibid., 135ff.

He wrote a play on "the subject of Our Lady of the Rosary," which he says was performed with "music on the flageolets." After this his success was assured and he was deluged with requests by "lovesick suitors ... sextons and wooers of nuns" and blind men.

The Spanish literature of the Baroque includes some interesting satirical references to the ancient tradition of the barber-musician. Quevedo, in his *The Vision of Hell*, discovers there the barbers who were well-known at this time as amateur players of the guitar.

> I passed along in the direction shown me, and saw—a punishment as astounding as it was just—that the barbers were all tied securely, but with their arms left free. Above their heads hung guitars and before them were boards set out with pieces for a game of draughts. When overcome by their natural inclination to strum a chord, like the typical street musicians they are, the barbers reached up for the guitars, the instrument were drawn up beyond their grasp; when they could no longer resist the temptation to take one of the pieces on the board before them, and put out a hand to do so, the boards sank down so that they could not touch them. This, then, was the punishment devised for barbers in Hell, and I could hardly leave the place where they were lodged for laughing at the spectacle.[34]

[34] Francisco de Quevedo, *Dreams and Discourses*, trans. R.K. Britton (Warminster: Aris & Phillips, 1989), 133ff.

Quevedo mentions these barber-musicians again in his "The Dream of Death." He sees "what seemed a group of infernal spirits, dragging with them chains of teeth, molars and incisors," whom he recognizes as dentists. Then he observes,

> Who, I asked myself, is likely to come forward to rub shoulders with this damnable rabble? for it seemed to me that a devil from Hell would be small beer in such accursed company. Then I heard a sudden outburst of guitar music, which cheered me somewhat since it was all *passacaglias* and *vacas*. May the grave claim me if it is not barbers making their entrance!, I exclaimed. It needed little by way of wit to confirm the fact. Barbers have *passacaglias* infused into their blood and are born with guitars in their hands. What a sight it was to behold them, some plucking some strumming, and I reflected that it was a dismal outlook for the beard that is trimmed to the strains of the guitar, likewise for the arm that is bled while performing a *chaconne* or a *folia*.[35]

[35] Ibid., 235.

Finally, there is a similar passage in Quevedo's noveletta, *The Dog & the Fever:*

> When I heard a great noise of guitars approaching, I felt a little cheered. All were playing lively music, *passacalles*, and *bacanalles*. May they kill me if it be not the surgeon barbers,

and they entering in. It was not difficult to tell that these people have *passacalles* infused into them, and the guitar as a natural gift. It was something to see the ones pluck and the others scrape the strings.[36]

[36] Don Francisco de Quevedo, *The Dog & the Fever,* trans. William Williams (Hamden, CT: Shoe String Press, 1954), 83ff.

Bibliography

Chapter 1 On Defining the Italian Baroque

Agazzari, Agostino. "On Playing upon a Bass in ... Consort." Quoted in Oliver Strunk, *Source Readings in Music History*. New York: Norton, 1950.

Berardi, Angelo. *Ragionamenti Musicali*. Bologna, 1681.

Bonachelli, Giovanni. *Corona di sacri gigli a una, due, tre, quattro, e cinque voci*. Venice, 1642.

Brett, Ursula. *Music and Ideas in Seventeenth Century Italy*. New York: Garland Publishing, 1989.

Burney, Charles. *Memoirs of the Life and Writings of the Abate Metastasio*. New York: Da Capo Press, 1971.

Cavalieri, Emilio de. "Rappresentazione di Anima, et di Corpo." Quoted in Carol MacClintock, *Readings in the History of Music in Performance*. Bloomington: Indiana University Press, 1979.

Cavicchi, A. "Inediti nell' episolario Vivaldi-Bentivoglio," *Nuova Rivista Musicale Italiana*, I (May/June, 1967).

Donnington, Robert. *The Interpretation of Early Music*. New York, 1964.

Frescobaldi, Girolamo. "Capricci fatti sopra diversi soggetti," quoted in Carol MacClintock, *Readings in the History of Music in Performance*. Bloomington: Indiana University Press, 1979

Gasparini, Francesco. *The Practical Harmonist at the Harpsichord* [1708]. Edited by Franks S. Stillings. New Haven: Yale School of Music, 1963.

Geminiani, Francesco. *A Treatise of Good Taste in the Art of Musick* [1749]. New York: Da Capo Press, 1969.

Kendall, Alan. *Vivaldi*. London: Granada Publishing, 1979.

Keysler, J. G. *Travels*. London, 1756.

Marcello, Benedetto. "Il teatro alla moda." Quoted in Oliver Strunk, *Source Readings in Music History*. New York: Norton, 1950.

Marino, Giambattista. *L'Adone* [1623]. Translated by Harold Priest. Ithaca: Cornell University Press, 1967.

Monteverdi, Claudio. *The Letters of Claudio Monteverdi*. Translated by Denis Stevens. Cambridge: Cambridge University Press, 1980.

———. "Madrigali guerrieri ed amorosi" [1638]. Quoted in Sam Morgenstern, *Composers on Music*. New York: Pantheon, 1956.

Morgenstern, Sam. *Composers on Music*. New York: Pantheon, 1956.

Palisca, Claude. *Baroque Music*. Englewood Cliffs: Prentice Hall, 1981.

Scarlatti, Alessandro. Letter to prince Ferdinand de' Medici, May 30, 1705. Quoted in Piero Weiss, *Letters of Composers Through Six Centuries*. Philadelphia: Chilton, 1967.

Strunk, Oliver. "François Raguenet, Comparison between the French and Italian Music (1702)." *The Musical Quarterly* 32, no. 4 (1946): 411–436.

Tosi, P. F. *Observations on the Florid Song*. London: Wilcox, 1743.

Trawick, Buckner. *World Literature*. New York: Barnes & Noble, 1955.

Weiss, Piero. *Letters of Composers Through Six Centuries*. Philadelphia: Chilton, 1967.

Chapter 2 Thoughts on the Beginning of Italian Opera

Addison, Joseph. *Remarks on Several Parts of Italy in 1701.* London, 1705.

Bianconi, Lorenzo. *Music in the Seventeenth Century.* Translated by David Bryant. Cambridge: Cambridge University Press, 1987.

Bukofzer, Manfred F. *Music in the Baroque Era.* New York: Norton, 1947.

Burney, Charles. *Memoirs of the Life and Writings of the Abate Metastasio.* New York: Da Capo Press, 1971.

Caccini. *Le Nuove Musiche.*

Evelyn, John. *Diary.* London, 1907.

Ferguson, Donald N. *A History of Musical Thought.* New York: Appleton-Century-Crofts, 1948.

Kendall, Alan. *Vivaldi.* London: Granada Publishing, 1979.

Misson, F. M. *A New Voyage to Italy.* London, 1695.

Monteverdi, Claudio. *The Letters of Claudio Monteverdi.* Translated by Denis Stevens. Cambridge: Cambridge University Press, 1980.

Palisca, Claude. *The Florentine Camerata.* New Haven: Yale University Press, 1989.

Pirrotta, Nino and Elena Povoledo. *Music and Theatre from Poliziano to Monteverdi.* Cambridge: Cambridge University Press, 1982.

Plato. *Gorgias.*

Plato. *Ion.*

Plato. *The Republic.* Translated by Benjamin Jowett.

Portnoy, Julius. *The Philosopher and Music.* New York: The Humanities Press, 1954.

Rosand, Ellen. "Venice, 1580–1680," In *The Early Baroque Era.* Englewood Cliffs: Prentice Hall, 1994.

Sainsbury, John. *Dictionary of Musicians.* London, 1825.

Strunk, Oliver. *Source Readings in Music History.* New York: Norton, 1950.

Chapter 3 Italian Views on Baroque Performance Practice

Agazzari, Agostino. *Del sonare sopra' l basso*. Siena, 1607. Quoted in Robert Donnington. *The Interpretation of Early Music*. New York, 1964.

———. Letter of 1606, quoted in Carol MacClintock, *Readings in the History of Music in Performance*. Bloomington: Indiana University Press, 1979.

———. Quoted in Oliver Strunk, *Source Readings in Music History*. New York: Norton, 1950.

Cerreto, Scipione. "Dell'arbore musicale" [Naples, 1608]. Quoted in Donnington, *The Interpretation of Early Music*. New York, 1964.

Doni, Giovanni Battista. "Trattati di musica" [1635]. Quoted in Robert Donnington, *The Interpretation of Early Music*. New York, 1964.

———. *Trattati di musica* [1635]. Edited A. F. Gori. Florence, 1763.

Frescobaldi, Girolamo. "Capricci fatti sopra diversi soggetti." Quoted in Carol MacClintock, *Readings in the History of Music in Performance*. Bloomington: Indiana University Press, 1979.

———. *Fiori musicali* [1635]. Quoted in Sam Morgenstern. *Composers on Music*. New York: Pantheon, 1956.

———. *Toccatas and Partitas*, Book I [1615].

———. "Toccate e partite d'intavolatura." Quoted in Carol MacClintock, *Readings in the History of Music in Performance*. Bloomington: Indiana University Press, 1979.

da Gagliano, Marco. "Dafne" [1608]. Quoted in Carol MacClintock, *Readings in the History of Music in Performance*. Bloomington: Indiana University Press, 1979.

Geminiani, Francesco. *A Treatise of Good Taste in the Art of Musick* [1749]. New York: Da Capo Press, 1969.

Grossi da Viadana, Lodovico. "Cento concerti ecclesiastici." Quoted in Oliver Strunk, *Source Readings in Music History*. New York: Norton, 1950.

Kendall, Alan. *Vivaldi*. London: Granada Publishing, 1979.

Lumsden, Alan. "Woodwind and Brass," in *Performance Practice: Music after 1600*. New York: Norton, 1989.

Maffei, Scipione. "Nuova Invenzione d'un Gravecembalo," in *Giornale dei Letterati d'Italia*. Venice, 1711.

Marcello, Benedetto. "Il treatro alla moda." Quoted in Oliver Strunk. *Source Readings in Music History*. New York: Norton, 1950.

Marino, Giambattista. *L'Adone* (1623). Translated by Harold Pries. Ithaca: Cornell University Press, 1967.

Monteverdi, Claudio. *The Letters of Claudio Monteverdi*. Translated by Denis Stevens. Cambridge: Cambridge University Press, 1980.

Morgenstern, Sam. *Composers on Music*. New York: Pantheon, 1956.

Strunk, Oliver. *Source Readings in Music History*. New York: Norton, 1950.

Tosi, P. F. *Observations on the Florid Song*. London: Wilcox, 1743.

della Valle, Pietro. "Della musica dell'età" [1640]. Quoted in Robert Donnington, *The Interpretation of Early Music*. New York, 1964.

Chapter 4 Kircher on Music

Hays, William. *Twentieth-Century Views of Music History*. New York: Scribner's, 1972.

Kircher, Athanasius. *Musurgia universalis* (1650). Translated by Frederick Crane (unpublished dissertation) State University of Iowa, 1956.

Chapter 5 On Court Music of the Italian Baroque

Bargagli, Scipione. *Della lodi dell' accademie* . . . . Florence, 1569.

Bianconi, Lorenzo. *Music in the Seventeenth Century*. Translated by David Bryant. Cambridge: Cambridge University Press, 1987.

Boyd, Malcolm. "Rome: the Power of Patronage." In *The Late Baroque Era*. Englewood Cliffs: Prentice Hall, 1994.

Brett, Ursula. *Music and Ideas in Seventeenth Century Italy.* New York: Garland Publishing, 1989.

Carter, Tim. "The North Italian Courts." In *The Early Baroque Era.* Englewood Cliffs: Prentice Hall, 1994.

Evelyn, John. *The Diary of John Evelyn.* Oxford, 1955.

Imbert, Gaetano. *La vita fiorentina nel '600.* Firenze, 1906.

Machiavelli. *The Art of War.*

Molmenti, Pompeo. *Venice.* London, 1908.

Monteverdi, Claudio. *The Letters of Claudio Monteverdi.* Translated by Denis Stevens. Cambridge: Cambridge University Press, 1980.

Nagler, A. M. *Theatre Festivals of the Medici.* (New Haven, 1964.

Nettl, Paul. "Equestrian Ballets of the Baroque Period." *The Musical Quarterly* 19, no. 1 (Jan., 1933): 74–83.

Saredo, Luisa. "Il Matrimonio di Vittorio Emanuele II su documenti inediti." In *Nuova Antologia* (1885).

Vessella, Alessandro. *La Banda.* Milan, 1935.

Chapter 6 On Civic and Military Music of the Italian Baroque

Abbatini, Antonio. [Poem], quoted in Lorenzo Bianconi. *Music in the Seventeenth Century.* Translated by David Bryant. Cambridge: Cambridge University Press, 1987.

Abbott, John S. C. *Italy.* New York, 1871.

Bianconi, Lorenzo. *Music in the Seventeenth Century.* Translated by David Bryant. Cambridge: Cambridge University Press, 1987.

Bontempi, Giovanni. *Historia musica.* Perugia, 1695.

Boyd, Malcolm. "Rome: the Power of Patronage." In *The Late Baroque Era.* Englewood Cliffs: Prentice Hall, 1994.

Brosses, Charles de. "Lettres familieres ecrites en Italie en 1739." Quoted in Carol MacClintock, *Readings in the History of Music in Performance.* Bloomington: Indiana University Press, 1979.

Grove, George. *Dictionary of Music.* (1980).

Hiller, J. A. *Lebensbeschreibungen berumter Musikgelehrten und Tonkunstler.* Leipzig, 1784.

Ivanovich, Cristoforo. [Diary]. Quoted in Lorenzo Bianconi. *Music in the Seventeenth Century.* Translated by David Bryant. Cambridge: Cambridge University Press, 1987.

Marzo, G. di. *Diario della citta di Palermo.*

Ottonelli, Giovan. *Cristiana moderazione del teatro* [1652].

Smithers, Don. *The Music and History of the Baroque Trumpet.* London: Dent.

Uberti, Grazioso. *Contrasto musico.* Quoted in Lorenzo Bianconi. *Music in the Seventeenth Century.* Translated by David Bryant. Cambridge: Cambridge University Press, 1987.

Vessella, Alessandro. *La Banda.* Milan, 1935.

Chapter 7 On Civic and Military Music of the Italian Baroque

Agazzari, Agostino. *On Playing upon a Bass in ... Consort.* Quoted in Oliver Strunk. *Source Readings in Music History.* New York: Norton, 1950.

Arnold, Denis. "Music at the Scuola de San Rocco." *Music & Letters* 40, no. 3 (Jul., 1959): 229-241.

Banchieri, Adriano. "Conclusioni nel suono dell' organo." Quoted in Lorenzo Bianconi. *Music in the Seventeenth Century.* Translated by David Bryant. Cambridge: Cambridge University Press, 1987.

Bartholomew, Leland. [Collection], Venice: Rauerij, 1608. Music Department, Fort Hays State College, Fort Hays, Kansas.

Bianconi, Lorenzo. *Music in the Seventeenth Century.* Translated by David Bryant. Cambridge: Cambridge University Press, 1987.

Brosses, Charles de. *Lettres familieres sur l'Italie.* Paris, 1931.

Donnington, Robert. *The Interpretation of Early Music.* New York, 1964.

Freschot, C. *Nouvelle relation de Venise.* Utrecht, 1709.

Giazotto, Remo. *Antonio Vivaldi.* Turin, 1973.

Giustiniani, Vicenzo. *Discorso sopra la Musica* [c. 1628]. Translated by Carol MacClintock. American Institute of Musicology, 1962.

Kendall, Alan. *Vivaldi*. London: Granada Publishing, 1979.

Kenton, Egon. *Life and Works of Giovanni Gabrieli*. American Institute of Musicology, 1967.

Kolneder, W. *Antonio Vivaldi, his life and work*. London, 1756.

Maugars, Andre. "Response faite a un curieux sur le Sentiment de la Musique d'Italie, Ecrite a Rome le premier Octobre 1639." Quoted in Carol MacClintock. *Readings in the History of Music in Performance*. Bloomington: Indiana University Press, 1979.

Marcello, Benedetto. *Il treatro alla moda*. Quoted in Oliver Strunk. *Source Readings in Music History*. New York: Norton, 1950.

Monteverdi, Claudio. *The Letters of Claudio Monteverdi*. Translated by Denis Stevens. Cambridge: Cambridge University Press, 1980.

Pincherle, Marc. "Vivaldi and the Ospitali of Venice." *The Musical Quarterly*, 24, no. 3 (Jul., 1938): 300–312.

Poellnitz, K. L. von. *Memoirs*. London, 1737.

Rousseau, J. J. *Confessions*.

Tosi, P. F. *Observations on the Florid Song*. London: Wilcox, 1743.

Venice, Archivio di Stato, Ospitali, busta 692, Notatorio Q, fol. 113r.

Chapter 8 Thoughts on Music of the Spanish Baroque

Calderon. *The Constant Prince*.
———. *The Great Theater of the World*.
———. *Life is a Dream*.
———. *Love after Death*.
———. *The Mayor of Zalamea*.
———. *The Painter of his Dishonor*.
———. *The Surgeon of Honor*.
Cerone, Domenico. *El Melopeo y Maestro* [1613].
Cunningham, Gilbert. *The Solitudes of Gongora*. Baltimore: Johns Hopkins Press, 1964.
Gongora, Luis. *First Solitude*.
Gracian, Baltasar. *The Oracle*.

———. *A Pocket Mirror for Heroes.*

Grove. *Dictionary of Music,* 1980.

Molina. *Damned for Despair.*

———. *Tamar's Revenge.*

———. *The Trickster of Seville.*

Nichols. *The Progresses of King James The First.* London, 1828.

Quevedo, Francisco de. *Dreams and Discourses.* Translated by R. K. Britton. Warminster: Aris & Phillips, 1989.

Quevedo, Francisco de. *Buscon.*

———. *The Dog & the Fever.*

———. *Dreams and Discourses.*

———. *The Dream of Death.*

———. *The Scavenger.*

———. *The Vision of Hell.*

Stein, Louise K. "The Iberian Peninsula." In *The Late Baroque Era.* Englewood Cliffs: Prentice Hall, 1994.

Torquemada, Juan de. Monarqu'a indiana. Quoted in Steven Barwick. "Mexico." In *The Early Baroque Era.* Englewood Cliffs: Prentice Hall, 1994.

Valdivielso. *The Bandit Queen.*

Vander Straeten, Edmond. *La Musique aux Pays-Bas.* New York, 1969.

About the Author

DR. DAVID WHITWELL is a graduate ("with distinction") of the University of Michigan and the Catholic University of America, Washington DC (PhD, Musicology, Distinguished Alumni Award, 2000) and has studied conducting with Eugene Ormandy and at the Akademie für Musik, Vienna. Prior to coming to Northridge, Dr. Whitwell participated in concerts throughout the United States and Asia as Associate First Horn in the USAF Band and Orchestra in Washington DC, and in recitals throughout South America in cooperation with the United States State Department.

At the California State University, Northridge, which is in Los Angeles, Dr. Whitwell developed the CSUN Wind Ensemble into an ensemble of international reputation, with international tours to Europe in 1981 and 1989 and to Japan in 1984. The CSUN Wind Ensemble has made professional studio recordings for BBC (London), the Köln Westdeutscher Rundfunk (Germany), NOS National Radio (The Netherlands), Zürich Radio (Switzerland), the Television Broadcasting System (Japan) as well as for the United States State Department for broadcast on its "Voice of America" program. The CSUN Wind Ensemble's recording with the Mirecourt Trio in 1982 was named the "Record of the Year" by *The Village Voice*. Composers who have guest conducted Whitwell's ensembles include Aaron Copland, Ernest Krenek, Alan Hovhaness, Morton Gould, Karel Husa, Frank Erickson and Vaclav Nelhybel.

Dr. Whitwell has been a guest professor in 100 different universities and conservatories throughout the United States and in 23 foreign countries (most recently in China, in an elite school housed in the Forbidden City). Guest conducting experiences have included the Philadelphia Orchestra, Seattle Symphony Orchestra, the Czech Radio Orchestras of Brno and Bratislava, The National Youth Orchestra of Israel, as well as resident wind ensembles in Russia, Israel, Austria, Switzerland, Germany, England, Wales, The Netherlands, Portugal, Peru, Korea, Japan, Taiwan, Canada and the United States.

He is a past president of the College Band Directors National Association, a member of the Prasidium of the International Society for the Promotion of Band Music, and was a member of the founding board of directors of the World Association for Symphonic Bands and Ensembles (WASBE). In 1964 he was made an honorary life member of Kappa Kappa Psi, a national professional music fraternity. In September, 2001, he was a delegate to the UNESCO Conference on Global Music in Tokyo. He has been knighted by sovereign organizations in France, Portugal and Scotland and has been awarded the gold medal of Kerkrade, The Netherlands, and the silver medal of Wangen, Germany, the highest honor given wind conductors in the United States, the medal of the Academy of Wind and Percussion Arts (National Band Association) and the highest honor given wind conductors in Austria, the gold medal of the Austrian Band Association. He is a member of the Hall of Fame of the California Music Educators Association.

Dr. Whitwell's publications include more than 127 articles on wind literature including publications in *Music and Letters* (London), the *London Musical Times*, the *Mozart-Jahrbuch* (Salzburg), and 50 books, among which is his 13-volume *History and Literature of the Wind Band and Wind Ensemble* and an 8-volume series on *Aesthetics in Music*. In addition to numerous modern editions of early wind band music his original compositions include five symphonies.

David Whitwell was named as one of six men who have determined the course of American bands during the second half of the twentieth century, in the definitive history, *The Twentieth Century American Wind Band* (Meredith Music). A doctoral dissertation by German Gonzales (2007, Arizona State University) is dedicated to the life and conducting career of David Whitwell through the year 1977. David Whitwell is one of nine men described by Paula A. Crider in *The Conductor's Legacy* (Chicago: GIA, 2010) as "the legendary conductors" of the twentieth century.

> "I can't imagine the 2nd half of the 20th century—without David Whitwell and what he has given to all of the rest of us."
> Frederick Fennell (1993)

About the Editor

CRAIG DABELSTEIN began studying the piano at age seven and took up the saxophone at age twelve. Mr Dabelstein has Bachelor of Arts (Music) and Bachelor of Music degrees from the Queensland Conservatorium of Music and a Graduate Diploma of Learning and Teaching and a Graduate Certificate in Editing and Publishing from the University of Southern Queensland. He has held the principal saxophone chairs in the Australian Wind Orchestra and has been an augmenting member of the Queensland Philharmonic and Symphony Orchestras. He was a member of the Queensland Saxophone Quartet and has previously been a saxophone teacher at the Queensland Conservatorium of Music. He is a regular conductor of the Queensland Wind Orchestra and has been a research associate for the *Teaching Music Through Performance in Band* series of books. He is the editor of more than forty books by Dr. David Whitwell including *A Concise History of the Wind Band, Foundations of Music Education, Music Education of the Future, The Sousa Oral History Project, Wagner on Bands, Berlioz on Bands, The Art of Musical Conducting, Aesthetics of Music* (8 volumes) and *The History and Literature of the Wind Band and Wind Ensemble* (13 volumes). He currently teaches saxophone and clarinet, and conducts bands at St Joseph's College, Gregory Terrace.

Books by David Whitwell

- The Sousa Oral History Project
- The Art of Musical Conducting
- The Longy Club: 1900–1917
- La Téléphonie and the Universal Musical Language
- Extraordinary Women
- A Concise History of the Wind Band
- Essays on the Modern Wind Band
- Essays on Performance Practice
- A New History of Wind Music
- The College and University Band
- The Early Symphonies of Mozart
- Band Music of the French Revolution
- Stories from the Podium

On Composers

- Wagner on Bands
- Berlioz on Bands
- Chopin: A Self-Portrait
- Liszt: A Self-Portrait
- Schumann: A Self-Portrait in His Own Words
- Mendelssohn: A Self-Portrait in His Own Words

On Education

- Philosophic Foundations of Education
- Foundations of Music Education
- Music Education of the Future

Aesthetics of Music

- Aesthetics of Music in Ancient Civilizations
- Aesthetics of Music in the Middle Ages
- Aesthetics of Music in the Early Renaissance
- Aesthetics of Music in Sixteenth-Century Italy, France and Spain
- Aesthetics of Music in Sixteenth-Century Germany, the Low Countries and England
- Aesthetics of Baroque Music in Italy, Spain, the German-Speaking Countries and the Low Countries
- Aesthetics of Baroque Music in France
- Aesthetics of Baroque Music in England

The History and Literature of the Wind Band and Wind Ensemble Series

- Volume 1 The Wind Band and Wind Ensemble Before 1500
- Volume 2 The Renaissance Wind Band and Wind Ensemble
- Volume 3 The Baroque Wind Band and Wind Ensemble
- Volume 4 The Wind Band and Wind Ensemble of the Classical Period (1750–1800)
- Volume 5 The Nineteenth-Century Wind Band and Wind Ensemble
- Volume 6 A Catalog of Multi-Part Repertoire for Wind Instruments or for Undesignated Instrumentation before 1600
- Volume 7 Baroque Wind Band and Wind Ensemble Repertoire
- Volume 8 Classical Period Wind Band and Wind Ensemble Repertoire
- Volume 9 Nineteenth-Century Wind Band and Wind Ensemble Repertoire
- Volume 10 A Supplementary Catalog of Wind Band and Wind Ensemble Repertoire
- Volume 11 A Catalog of Wind Repertoire before the Twentieth Century for One to Five Players
- Volume 12 A Second Supplementary Catalog of Early Wind Band and Wind Ensemble Repertoire
- Volume 13 Name Index, Volumes 1–12, The History and Literature of the Wind Band and Wind Ensemble

Ancient Voices

- Ancient Views on Music and Religion
- Ancient Views on the Natural World
- Ancient Views on What Is Music
- Contemporary Descriptions of Early Musicians
- Early Views of Music and Ethics
- Early Thoughts on Performance Practice
- Music Performance in Ancient Societies

Renaissance Voices

- Essays on Renaissance Philosophies of Music
- Renaissance Men on Music

www.whitwellbooks.com

www.ingramcontent.com/pod-product-compliance
Lightning Source LLC
Chambersburg PA
CBHW080452170426
43196CB00016B/2776